How to Run Your Own
Restaurant

How to Run Your Own
Restaurant

**Bingley Sim
and William Gleeson**

KOGAN
PAGE

Kogan Page Limited
120 Pentonville Road
London N1 9JN

© Bingley Sim and William Gleeson 1994

British Library Cataloguing in Publication Data

A CIP record for this book is available from the British Library.

ISBN 0-7494-1031-0

Typeset by DP Photosetting, Aylesbury, Bucks
Printed and bound in Great Britain by
Clays Ltd, St Ives plc

For my mum,
G.T. Geh,

the best cook
in the world

Bingley Sim
January 1994

United Kingdom telephone numbers are due to change on 16 April 1995. After that date, please check any numbers in this book that you plan to use.

Contents

Chapter 1
Introduction

Your dream

Who hasn't thought of running their own restaurant at some time? Maybe you enjoy entertaining friends at dinner parties, maybe you enjoy going out to restaurants but can't help thinking that you could have made a tastier dish, prepared a more daring menu, created a more individual atmosphere. Running your own restaurant can be one of the most satisfying ways of making a living. It allows for creativity, artistic expression and ingenuity, and also competition, inspiration and sheer hard work. It is often the last element that deters people from ever living their dream.

It is true that running a restaurant is hard work. It is one of the most volatile industries and your local high street will no doubt bear witness to restaurants which threw open their doors in a wave of excitement, only to board them up with a For Sale sign a few months later. But there are also those which stood the test of time and cornered a market, became part of the locality's character.

There are nearly 15,000 restaurant businesses in the UK, employing around 300,000 people. The recession of the early 1990s and the huge fall in consumer spending have meant that nearly all restaurants have experienced a drop in turnover, and many have gone under, particularly those which over-expanded in the boom years of the 1980s. It has been a difficult time for restaurateurs, but the recession has had the benefit of rooting out the weak, making prices more realistic, and premises are now cheaper to rent or buy.

Running a restaurant means total dedication, working all hours, and it will play havoc with your social life – you only have to think of the many TV sit-coms such as *Chef!* or the classic *Fawlty Towers* to realise this. There are risks and uncertainties and the danger of failure, but if you never take the risk, your dream will remain a dream and not reality.

To realise your dream you need to have a thorough understanding of the profession and a meticulous plan as to how your restaurant will operate. This book will analyse why some restaurants succeed and others fail, and help you to give your business the best chance of being one of the successes.

The ingredients of success

No one becomes a successful restaurateur overnight by magic. Whether the restaurant survives will depend primarily on how profitable it is at the end of the day, and to be profitable you must have designed your restaurant so that it appeals to your chosen market, and you must have planned your business so that it runs efficiently and smoothly. Many restaurateurs make the mistake of trying to manage the finances without sufficient knowledge until it is too late, and many good restaurants have failed for simply this reason alone. If you do not have an acumen for figures, get professional help at the outset. Chapter 7 looks at how to choose your professional advisers and make them work for you. The book will also consider the following vital ingredients for success:

- Choosing the right locality for the type of restaurant you want to run – Chapter 2
- Selecting the most appropriate form of business vehicle – Chapter 2
- Financing your restaurant – Chapter 3
- The ins and outs of franchising – Chapter 4
- Managing the finances and tax – Chapter 5
- The secrets of successful marketing and advertising – Chapter 6
- Employing staff – Chapter 8
- Satisfying legal requirements – Chapter 9
- Design and layout of the kitchen – Chapter 11
- Knowing your food and drink, and the daily operations of running a restaurant – Chapters 10 and 12.

You will also need to examine yourself – your personality and strengths and weaknesses – to see if running a restaurant is the right business for you.

What makes a successful restaurateur?

A good restaurateur, first and foremost, has a love of food and drink. He or she is a *bon viveur* who delights in the company of others and creates an ambience of comfort and pleasure. A good knowledge of wine will be needed in order to recommend a vintage that would complement a particular dish. A genuine interest in and appreciation of food will ensure good quality control and a varied and appealing menu. You may have come by this knowledge from your own experience of entertaining and dining out, or you may consider taking a course in food and drink and cookery or work in a restaurant as a cook or waiter and observe the day-to-day running of the outlet.

Some experience of working in a restaurant will give you an insight into the energy and effort required to run a successful establishment and it will help you to develop a sense of what appeals to customers and what does not. The saying 'the customer is always right' is more true in the restaurant business than in any other. After all, if the customers do not like what's on offer, they will vote with their feet and not come back.

As you will know from personal experience, the customer comes to a restaurant not just to satisfy hunger but for entertainment and relaxation. You must learn to assess your customers and their needs. Are the couple looking for a quiet table for a romantic dinner? Does this customer wish to impress his colleagues with a stylish dinner over which they will finalise important decisions? How can you ensure that Dad gives his kids a jolly day out, the daughter treats her mother, the party-goers party, and the traveller to town finds rest and comfort? Besides designing your restaurant to meet the needs of your customers, you will also listen to your customers and make an effort to remember their names, and they will return and bring new customers with them. Personal recommendation is one of the surest forms of advertising, and, who knows, the next customer whose conversation you find scintillating, and whose every need is your command, may just be a restaurant critic!

You must be open to change so that your restaurant develops and grows to meet the varying tastes of your customers, and you must pop in the odd surprise to challenge and interest the diners as well. But most of all you must hold on to your dream and feed it with energy and enthusiasm, because ultimately running a restaurant is about having fun and making others have fun too. If you are sure of your dream – however humble its beginnings – you will inspire your staff to ensure a smooth run and safe business. Your knowledge and understanding of the business, the operations of the market and the requirements of the law will help to ensure this. Running a restaurant is a way of life. You will become known in your community. What can bring more pleasure than seeing regulars returning and new customers discovering you? You are your own boss and can realise your own ideas and innovations. You can decide what your restaurant will look like, who you will employ, what wines you will offer, what special offer to tempt people with, and how your business will grow. With good planning and careful management, your dream will not only become a reality, but could well be very lucrative and enjoyable.

So stop dreaming – read on, and get nearer to when your doors open for the first time and the customers come flooding in!

Chapter 2

Setting Up a Restaurant Business

In this chapter we look at two fundamental aspects of starting up your restaurant business: location of the premises, and the legal form of the business. It is most important that all statutory requirements are met.

Location

Desirable locations, such as a busy high street, or a well-established area of restaurant and other entertainment facilities, are always more expensive than out of the way places. This is true whether you rent or buy your premises. However, the location should be considered as an investment in the business. Location will affect how easily you can attract customers. For example, if you are near a cinema or pub, you may attract customers from there, or if you are in a busy shopping area, you will have hungry shoppers at lunch time looking for a quick bite, or local residents seeking a pleasant evening out. This in turn will influence the sort of menu you offer. Location, the type of customers and the menu must all be compatible.

You should consider the following points when choosing your location:

- *Cost:* do you have adequate finance to rent or buy the premises?
- *Competitors:* what is the competition now, and what might it be in the future? Can you compete?
- *Type of restaurant:* are you hoping to target residential evening customers or lunch-time business trade? The location must be selected accordingly.
- *Parking facilities:* ample car parking is an attraction to many customers, particularly in busy towns or cities.

- *Planning permissions:* do the premises already have a licence to trade as a restaurant, or will you need to apply for one? Will any alterations to the building be necessary?
- *Character of area:* this must be in keeping with the type of restaurant you want to set up. A bustling high street or local shopping area is ideal for cheap and simple meals, an exotic and pricey menu will need to be in a well-off residential or business area.
- *Proximity to your home:* you will spend a lot of time at the restaurant and this will involve many early starts and late nights. You may also need to reach your restaurant quickly in emergencies.

Research is vital – and can be fun too! Simple market surveys such as ordering a meal from a potential competitor is very revealing. What are the meal and service like? Will yours be better? Count and scrutinise the customers. Are there enough? Are they there for a quick bite, or to eat well and socialise?

Investigate all the different restaurants and take-aways and make a note of the sorts of menu and their price ranges. Will your business compete or fill a gap in the market? If the location is new to you, talk to the locals and ask them what sort of restaurant they would like. Buy the local newspaper to get a feel of the area, and check the adverts for restaurants and take-aways.

Contact the local council to enquire about business rates. Assess the business rates and activities in the area: will office workers want a light lunch, will business people want to entertain clients, are there local school children or college students around or shoppers?

Type of premises

The first decision is whether to acquire a property already set up as a restaurant, or convert a property into a restaurant. There are advantages and disadvantages to each, but if you are new to the restaurant business and finances are limited, it is often easier to acquire a property that has been or is used for catering purposes. Installing a completely new restaurant with cooking facilities and dining area with refreshment facilities is far more expensive than making alterations to an existing restaurant. If the site is not used for catering purposes, it will probably not have permission to trade as a restaurant. You will have to obtain this permission from the town planner of the local council, involving extra time and expense and professional fees. If the site is unsuitable for the restaurant trade, permission will be refused.

The advantage of setting up a restaurant from scratch is that you have much more freedom to design and a restaurant adds value to a building so you should be able to acquire the property more cheaply. When it comes to selling your property its value will have increased considerably.

Renting or buying

Buying a property outright will almost certainly involve more expense than renting it, but being the sole owner has many advantages. You will be able to remain in the property for as long as you wish. It is often difficult to 'take customers with you' when you move site. Having no landlord, you will not have to seek permission to do anything to the property apart from the usual planning permission from your local council. However, you will be solely responsible for all repair and maintenance and other expenses associated with owning property.

Renting is the more common option. If you are giving the restaurant a trial go, it is less daunting to commit yourself to a short lease than to buy a property. A sum of money will be required 'up front' but otherwise rent is usually paid at regular intervals, such as yearly, quarterly or monthly. There are currently many incentives to encourage business growth, such as 'rent free' periods, sometimes of more than a year.

The actual lease will be a detailed document and it is essential that you obtain a good solicitor to negotiate favourable terms for you. The lease will cover all aspects of the property, in particular alterations, repairs and maintenance, and use of the property and provisions for renewing or terminating the lease. Be sure that you are fully aware of your responsibilities and that you comply with them or you may be at risk of the landlord terminating your lease. Some leases can be very restrictive. For example, if the landlord owns a number of properties together, he may stipulate certain opening times so that the area is always busy at the same time, thus generating more trade. Rent is sometimes set as a fixed sum plus a percentage of the quarter's turnover. This is helpful when business is slow, but can be a drain on a thriving business.

You and your solicitor should satisfy yourselves that your landlord is a responsible and soundly financed individual or business. Most disputes arise from repairs being delayed, or punitive rent rises. If there are other tenants, talk to them. Do they run a tenants' association which has some power to influence the landlord's actions and which shares common expenses? Often common expenses such as communal lighting, heating, cleaning and security are paid for by the landlord levying a regular service charge. Find out how much this usually is, and what controls there are to ensure that the landlord does not set exorbitant charges.

A lease will commit you to a certain term of renting the property, and you will be liable for the rent during this entire period. Consider carefully whether you need a 'break clause' which enables you to end the lease after a specified time if you want to, or whether you can assign your lease to another (in effect sell the lease) or sub-let the property (allow another business to move in as your own tenant and receive rent from them).

Be certain that you can renew the lease or extend it if you wish. Your solicitor will advise you whether the property comes under the law that enables tenants to demand new leases in certain circumstances (the Landlord and Tenant Act 1954), or whether the landlord insists that you agree beforehand that the Act will not apply.

A good solicitor is essential. Currently, because of the effects of the last recession, all terms are negotiable, and you need to be sure that you get the best bargain you can. There are many bargains – take a look at your local newspaper and enquire at the estate agents.

Alterations to the premises

If you want to renovate or extend the premises or the shop-front or even just the signboard, you need to check whether planning permission is needed from the town council and/or from your landlord. Though some alterations can be made without formal application, it is imperative to check before-hand. If work which requires planning permission has been started without approval being obtained, the local planning authority can serve an enforcement notice which will require the building to be returned to its original state.

An architect is required to draw up complete plans of the proposed work for submission to the local planning office.

Also check to ensure whether the shop is in a Conservation Area, or whether it is a Listed Building of architectural or historic interest, or affected by a special condition on an earlier planning permission. Check with the local council planning department because different rules will apply in these circumstances.

Building regulations

Approval under the building regulations has to be obtained to ensure that the buildings are renovated in the correct manner and with the right materials. Moreover, the structural chan-ges need to be in line with fire regulations: suitable means of escape in case of fire are always needed. For some premises this will involve two exits and fire-proof lobbies. Building regulations are separate from the planning controls; there-fore, approval from the building regulations does not auto-matically mean that planning permission is obtained.

Legal restrictions

Check whether there are any covenants in your lease or by-laws which alter your plans. Covenants can exist between freeholders of land, and between landlord and tenant, and the tenant and other tenants. Positive covenants oblige the covenantee to do something to fulfil the covenant, such as maintain a party wall. Restrictive covenants prohibit the carrying out of specific events. The covenants may be expressly written into the conveyance or lease, or they may be implied by custom or law. If the covenant is breached you will be liable for damage. Your solicitor will be able to enquire whether you may be released from the covenant.

Changing the type of shop

If you purchased a shop which has not got A3 use permission (premises used for sale of food for consumption on the premises), you will need to obtain permission. You will have to pay a fee and the council normally takes about two months to reach a decision.

Shop-front and signs

Planning permission is needed if you wish to alter your shop-front. Canopies which project in the front need approval. Signboards come under the advertisement regulations. Changing the name does not need permission but if you wish to use illuminated signs, consent is required. However, if the previous shop already had an illuminated sign and you do not plan to change the surface area of type illumination but just the name, permission is not normally required but separate permission to erect signs may be needed under the lease.

Demolition

Though you do not normally need planning permission to demolish part of the premises, you will certainly need planning permission to rebuild. Before demolition work begins, it is advisable to ensure that what is to be demolished is not part of your neighbour's premises. This is not always easy when party walls are in question. Demolition will obviously require consent from the landlord if the premises are leasehold.

A step-by-step guide to planning permission

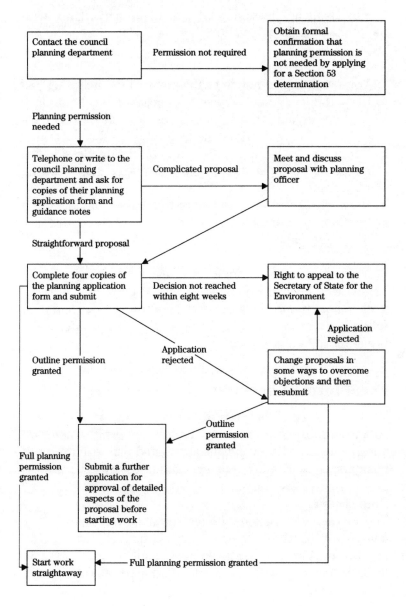

Licensing application procedures

The licensing application must be made in accordance with the procedures laid down in Schedule 2 of the Licensing Act 1964:

1. You need to give notice to the clerk to the licensing justices, the local chief officer of police, the local authority and the fire authority. This must be done at least 21 days before the date fixed for the Licensing Sessions hearing.
2. For a 28-day period before the Licensing Sessions, a notice of the application must be displayed at or near the restaurant.
3. Between 14 and 28 days before the date of the Licensing Sessions, you need to advertise a copy of the notice in a local newspaper.

If, however, you are taking over a restaurant which already possesses a licence, you need to give 21 days' notice to the licence holder informing the person of the transfer and then follow only procedure (1) above. You need not inform the fire authority on this occasion.

Legal form of business

There are three main types of business you can trade as: a sole trader, a partnership or a limited company. There are advantages and disadvantages associated with each form of business, as well as different legal and statutory implications.

Sole trader
This is when you carry on the restaurant business personally and on your own. There is no legal distinction between you and the business. You will have no limit to your personal liability, and so will be responsible for paying all the debts of the business.

The main advantages of being a sole trader are:

1. The cost of formation is low.
2. You are taxed on profits and not on drawings.

3. The accounts of the business need not be audited or filed with the Registrar of Companies. The cost of meeting these requirements can be considerable.
4. Tax advantages in the early years of trading.
5. The correct accounting date would ensure further tax savings in later years.
6. There is greater flexibility in obtaining relief for trading losses, especially in the early years of trading, as there is a special relief for losses incurred in the first four years of trading.

For more details about the tax matters referred to above, you should contact your accountant.

The disadvantages of being a sole trader are:

1. You are personally liable for all the business debts.
2. If the restaurant is highly profitable you will be liable to higher rate tax as it is not possible to retain the profits in the business.
3. It is usually more difficult to raise capital.

Partnership

A partnership is when two or more people carry on a business with a view to profit. There is no legal requirement that a partnership be regulated by a partnership deed, though it is strongly advisable that a deed is drawn up. A properly drafted partnership deed should contain articles regulating:

(a) the running of the business;
(b) the financing of the partnership as well as determining the profit share and remuneration of each partner;
(c) the rights and duties of the partners;
(d) the termination of the partnership.

If a partnership deed is not drawn up, the Partnership Act 1890 will be assumed to apply instead. This will impose a number of provisions including:

(a) the profits and losses are shared equally;
(b) all decisions require unanimous support;

(c) capital gains and losses are shared in the profit-sharing ratio;

(d) the partnership continues until dissolved and any partner may dissolve the partnership at any time.

As any partnership (including a husband and wife team) can involve considerable financial commitment, it is advisable to speak to a solicitor first.

Advantages of a partnership
In addition to the advantages of being a sole trader, other advantages are:

(a) Partnership salaries can be used to maximise the tax efficiency of personal allowances, especially in a husband and wife team. This is also the case even if one spouse is not as involved in the running of the business.

(b) A sole trader who has had several years of high profits can minimise tax liabilities by bringing a partner into the business.

Disadvantages of a partnership
The disadvantages of being a sole trader are also applicable to a partnership. In addition:

(a) Partners share the liability for each partner's action.

(b) The more partners there are, the greater the likelihood of disagreements which may lead to the dissolution of the partnership.

Limited company
A limited company has a separate legal existence from its directors or shareholders, and is therefore able to trade and be responsible for all its own actions. It has its own legal personality. Limited companies are governed by the Companies Act as well as a number of other specific legislations.

Advantages of a limited company
(a) The liability of the shareholders is limited to the amount of share capital allotted.

(b) Profits can be retained within the business and do not have to be distributed to the shareholders.

(c) It is easier to spread the value of the company around the family.

(d) There is more scope for tax planning, especially pension provision.

Disadvantages of a limited company

(a) All drawings taken out as salary will be subject to immediate taxation and National Insurance.

(b) The benefit of limited liability is nowadays not really relevant because personal guarantees are required by banks and landlords.

(c) The audited accounts have to be prepared and professional costs can be considerable.

(d) Accounts and shareholdings have to be filed with the Registrar and the public has access to them.

(e) Higher formation costs.

In practice, a restaurant business usually starts as a sole trader and as business expands this will lead to the incorporation of the business for commercial reasons. From a taxation point of view, the rule of thumb for a sole trader or partnership is to keep profits in the first accounting period to a legal minimum. Some ways of doing this include:

(a) leasing the assets rather than buying them;

(b) borrowing initial capital as all the interest is allowable for tax;

(c) undertaking all necessary repairs and renewals work in the first accounting period.

Checklist of statutory requirements

- Notify the local Tax Inspector that you are starting your restaurant. The address of your local Tax Office appears in the local telephone directory under Inland Revenue.
- Inform the Department of Social Security for National Insurance contributions purposes.
- Notify the Inland Revenue of your intention to operate the PAYE system.

- Register your business for VAT with the local Customs and Excise. Your local VAT Office is in the phone book under Customs and Excise.
- Certificate of employers' liability to be prominently displayed.
- You should decide whether or not to engage an accountant (see Chapter 7).

Opening a bank account

It is advisable to open your business account close to either your home or the restaurant. You will be obliged to have your account with the bank which has given you loan and overdraft facilities.

You have to decide who will be the cheque signatories when completing the bank mandate form. Ask your bank manager to send you regular bank statements, preferably weekly.

Business name

You will probably want to trade under a business name which promotes an image for your restaurant and is attractive and easy to remember. However, when a business name is used, you have to comply with regulations.

Since 1982, anyone trading under a name other than their own surname has to disclose the name of the proprietor of the business. A partnership must disclose the names of all the partners, and a company, the full corporate name. In each case you will also need to have a business or other address such as your accountant's or your solicitor's to which official documents may be served. This is known as the Registered Office.

If any customer asks for the name and address of the owner, these must be supplied immediately in writing. This information is usually disclosed on the business stationery. It is a criminal offence to fail to comply with the regulations and offenders are liable to be fined.

Stationery

Letters, invoices and mailshots are effective ways of advertising. You have to consider legal requirements when you design your stationery.

	Limited company	*Partnership*	*Sole trader*
Letters	Name of company	Names of all the partners	Own name
	Country of registration		Business address
	Address of registered office	Principal office of the partnership	
Invoices	Name of company	VAT registration number	VAT registration number
	Company registration number		
	VAT registration number		
	Names of *all* the directors or none		

Checklist of other services required

- Credit card registration (usually takes more than a month).
- Electricity.
- Gas.
- Telephone and fax.
- Council rates (local authority).
- Drop into your local police station. It certainly helps to be friendly with your local police as you never know when you might need their service.

As the law is constantly changed and added to, you must contact your solicitor or your accountant to ensure that you comply fully with the latest requirements.

Chapter 3
Raising Capital

In this chapter we look at sources of funds for the initial investment, and how to convince the owners of those sources that your business represents a good opportunity for them. You will need to produce a detailed business plan, outlining your finance, assets, products, markets and staff. This business plan is necessary for two reasons:

1. Any investor will require a business plan which indicates that the business is a good investment.
2. For your own purposes, you will need to evaluate whether the investment of your money and time will be worth while.

A business plan consists of two main elements:

1. The marketing plan. This will include:

    - *Market size and potential:* for instance, who your customers are, and whether the market is growing;
    - *Marketing and sales methods* of reaching your customers, whether through advertising, mailshots, leafleting etc;
    - *List of competing restaurants,* their prices and market share.

2. The financial forecasts. They will include:

    - *Expected turnover for the year;*
    - *Sales break-even:* in other words, how much the restaurant must take in before a profit is made;
    - *Cash flow forecast:* your estimate of the movement of cash in the business.

The assumptions that you make in the computations must be clearly spelled out in notes to the forecasts.

Other elements of the business plan will include:

- a general introductory narrative which will include information on the scale of the restaurant;
- a description of the operation and the required staff levels;
- your personal details, and those of others involved in managing the business. Remember to emphasise any previous business and catering experience.

A business plan is ultimately an estimate, a series of best guesses about the future. As such, it may turn out that the estimates differ from the eventual results of the restaurant. Nevertheless, it is possible to predict the future carefully. For example, if you plan to rent premises in a certain part of town, you should contact an estate agent who specialises in that area, and ask what the going rate per square foot is for the sort of premises you have in mind. If you are planning a prime site location, don't use an estimate for side street premises. If you have a particular site in mind, contact the landlord or his agent and ask about the rent. In the notes to the business plan, make the source of your estimates clear.

Where all the amounts in the business plan are thought through carefully, it should be possible to predict the likely trading performance of the restaurant accurately.

We will look at an example of a business plan at the end of this chapter. First, it is necessary to consider, as comprehensively as possible, the start-up costs and running costs that the initial investment will have to meet.

Start-up costs

The list below is thorough, but there may be other costs associated with your particular restaurant which you will need to include as well.

Building and business

- Capital cost or premium on the lease

- Goodwill
- Deposits
- Rent in advance
- Legal and survey fees (it is also common to bear the vendor's solicitor's fees)
- Business rates
- Alteration to premises
- Other costs including sign writing, insurance etc.

Plant, machinery, fixtures and fittings

- Furniture, including new signs
- Kitchen equipment
- Alterations to kitchen, eg stoves and fridges
- Crockery and glasses
- Purchase of van.

Stock

- Purchase of stock including wine
- Leaflets and take-away menus
- Business cards.

Staffing

- Initial wages and salaries
- Staff uniforms.

Financing expenses

- Professional fees (in arrangement of loans)
- Interest on capital.

Sources of capital

For many people with no business experience, the sourcing of investment into a small private business is one of the great mysteries of life. Be assured that there are many sources of capital, some quite close to home, while others involve complete strangers. The source you eventually get your capital from will, in part, depend on your personal circum-stances, and may include:

- You and your family
- Your friends and relatives
- Trading partners
- Banks
- Government assistance
- Trade credits
- Hire purchase and leasing
- Business angels.

You and your family

This is the easiest way of raising capital and probably the cheapest means of doing so.

- Savings and investments
- Endowment policies
- Remortgage of property.

You must, however, be wary of the possibility that the business may fail, in which case your lifetime savings will be lost.

Your friends and relatives

Although this is a cheap way of raising capital, you have to ensure that the terms of the repayments are agreed and, if necessary, legally drawn up to prevent future disagreement.

Trading partners

If any of your trading partners is willing to inject capital into the business, a number of points have to be agreed. You need to decide whether interest is payable on the capital or if the injection of capital is an entitlement to a share of the profits.

Banks

Borrowing from the high street banks used to be the conventional source of money. However, the banks have become reluctant lenders in the last few years, following the unprecedented level of business failures. The banks require a detailed business plan and cash flow forecast before they consider lending the money.

The banks prefer to share the risk of a restaurant business and would expect you to put up a large proportion of the capital. It is also common for them to ask for security on the loans made; for instance, a charge on the property, assurance policies or your own home.

There are two usual types of bank borrowing:

1. *Overdrafts.* These are for short-term working capital and usually at favourable terms (depending on how friendly the bank manager is). Unlike a loan, the overdraft may be withdrawn at any time, usually at the manager's discretion. It is therefore advisable to keep within the limits laid down by the bank.
2. *Loans.* Most loans are for a fixed period at an agreed rate of interest. Even though the interest rate charge is normally fixed at several percentage points above the base lending rate, it is possible to negotiate a more favourable interest rate.

It is normal for most restaurant businesses to have a combination of both an overdraft facility and a fixed loan.

Government assistance

Under the Loan Guarantee Scheme the government will guarantee up to 70 per cent (85 per cent in certain inner city areas) of the loan over two to seven years. In return you need to pay a premium of 2.5 per cent on the total sum borrowed.

The government also has schemes to help long-term unemployed people by subsidising the wages of the staff employed during the training period.

Trade credits

Try to get as long a credit period as possible from your suppliers, even though they are usually unwilling to give much credit to someone with whom they have just started trading.

Hire purchase and leasing

There are a number of finance companies which are willing to purchase the equipment and then sell the equipment on a hire purchase agreement or lease the equipment back to the business. The equipment remains the property of the finance companies until the lease or hire purchase has been repaid.

You must be careful when you sign the agreement because the contractual obligation of the finance lease generally cannot be cancelled. It is also important to know if the lease is a finance or operating lease because, if it is an operating lease, the lessor (the finance company) retains the owner-ship as well as assuming responsibility for repairs, maintenance and insurance.

The costs involved are usually higher than bank loans.

Business angels

The business angel phenomenon is relatively new. It involves matching an entrepreneur's investment capital needs with wealthy private individuals seeking a good, high return investment. The British Venture Capital Association runs a 'marriage bureau' matching prospective investments with wealthy investors.

Often the investor chooses activities of which he has experience. This form of investment can be linked to the tax-efficient Enterprise Investment Scheme, set up in the November 1993 Budget, which, unlike the now defunct Business Expansion Scheme, allows investors to participate in the management of the business.

The advantages of this scheme are that you will raise your money and benefit from the management experience of the investor. The main disadvantages are the cost (the investor may want half your profits initially) and the fact that you will lose some control over your business.

A sample business plan

A good business plan has the following characteristics:

1. *Concise.* Not verbose or too speculative about the distant future.
2. *Substantial.* All the assumptions must have some evidence or research to support them. Use as many photographs and documents as are relevant.
3. *Comprehensive.* All details should be fully considered for at least the first 12 months, and up to three years ahead.

4. *Objective.* The purpose of a business plan is not to justify your preconceived ideas. A good plan will also include a worst case scenario; in other words, be realistic about the chance of success for your restaurant.

A business plan must have, at the very least, the following sub-sections:

1. *Introduction about the restaurant.* Outline the type of food and services that your restaurant will provide, where it will be located and what differentiates it from the local competition. Mention the market research you have carried out.
2. *Owners and key personnel.* Their curricula vitae, detailing age, qualifications and experience of management and the catering trade. For many outside investors, this will be the crucial section by which they will judge your business.
3. *The marketing summary.* Describe and define the market you will serve. Research will also determine the socio-economic factors affecting the restaurant, as well as the types of customer who will patronise the place. You also need to mention in detail your major competitors, how your prices compare with theirs and how you plan to do better than them. Your marketing strategies should also be summarised.
4. *Financial forecasts.* This will include a budgeted profit and loss account and a cash flow statement. It will also include explanatory notes justifying amounts used in the forecasts.

   It is advisable to underestimate your sales rather than overestimate them. Likewise, it is better to overestimate your costs. You should prepare alternative cash flow forecasts, using best and worst scenarios as this will help to identify financial needs at each extreme. This will also enable you to arrange emergency funds and facilities from the beginning rather than when the requirement suddenly arises.
5. *Investment required.* You need to list all your start-up costs, showing the estimated amount for each one. Having worked out the total finance required, you should then list

how you propose to raise the capital. This will actually show the amount that you hope to borrow from the prospective lender.

Even if you are using entirely your own capital, you should at least do the budgeted profit and loss and cash flow statements. You can then assess how much you will need to invest to start the business and keep it afloat in the initial stages. The worst possible scenario is to start a profitable business only to be unable to sustain interest payments or not meet your tax bills because of lack of funds and planning.

Examples of a budgeted profit and loss account and a cash flow statement are shown in Chapter 5.

Chapter 4
Franchising

As we have seen in the previous chapters, there are many factors that determine whether a restaurant will be a success. A lot of skill and knowledge is needed in order to make the right choices, and you must be in full control of the finances and administration. Franchising reduces some of these responsibilities, and lessens the risks. A restaurant which has just opened must develop its reputation and this takes time. A franchise has a ready-made reputation with a proven market. A franchise can be lucrative, and it can also be a useful way of gaining the necessary experience to go it alone.

What is franchising?

Most well-known restaurant chains such as McDonald's and Pizza Express operate franchises. A franchise is a contractual licence which allows an individual, the franchisee, to use the name and image of the franchisor in return for a fee. The franchisor will assist in the organisation of the business, the selection of premises, training, marketing and merchandising. The franchisor will be keen to ensure that all outlets are run similarly so that the standard of quality is upheld and customers can easily identify the particular restaurant.

The franchisee has to pay a capital sum, and a management fee or royalties usually based on a percentage of the gross income of the outlet. Often the franchisee is under an obligation to purchase specified brands of products or services.

The whole aim of franchising is that each outlet mutually profits from the reputation of the others. In this way, a name will have an impact on the market. People will easily recognise the restaurant by its name and appearance and they will know what to expect of its quality. The idea is that, rather than take a risk on an unknown restaurant, people will choose something familiar, and they will be reassured by the knowledge that the food will be the same whether it is in Edinburgh or Exeter.

Advantages and disadvantages

The most obvious advantage is that the risk of failure is reduced. The image and products are already known to the public, the market research has been carried out, and the popularity of the type of outlet has been proved. Besides reassuring you, this will also reassure banks and other lending institutions and individuals should you need to raise capital. It should be possible to obtain a favourable loan rate in view of the fact that your franchise business will be less risky than a completely new venture.

If you have no experience of working in a restaurant and do not have any contacts in the business on whom you can call, the ready-made structure of a franchise is very helpful. The franchisor will assist with the management of the restaurant and the training of the staff. The disadvantage is that this sort of involvement can feel intrusive and restrictive. Your freedom in how you run the restaurant will be limited. Most franchises have uniformly fitted out premises and standard menus.

As your restaurant will be one of many, the franchisor will help with advertising. Local advertising will alert customers to the presence of your outlet in their area. National advertising is also effective owing to the fact that the franchises are all similar to each other. Advertising is an important element in a restaurant's success, so the power and effectiveness of a national advertising campaign are useful. However, you may also have ideas of your own for promoting your restaurant. Often your franchise contract will restrict you from doing your own promotions as prices are usually standard in each outlet. If one restaurant is doing a special offer, so will all the others, making the offer somewhat less special!

As a franchisee, you will have to compete only with other restaurants and different franchises. Another same name franchisee will not be allowed to set up a business in direct competition to yours in your vicinity as you will be given exclusive territorial rights.

Another aspect of being part of a large organisation is that you may be able to buy cheaper goods and materials through the franchisor than as an individual. This is not always the case, however, and your contract may oblige you to purchase specified brands, even if you can find cheaper elsewhere; this obligation will also restrict your individuality as you will not be able to branch out into buying different goods or goods of a more up-market quality.

Good advertising is always good for business, but bad advertising can be disastrous. As franchises are seen by the public as a single product even though they are, in fact, run by franchisees independent of each other, bad publicity for one outlet will mean bad publicity for everyone. A food poisoning scare in London could affect your turnover even if you are based in Cardiff, or a news story about bad staff relations in one area could make hiring staff for your restaurant more difficult.

A franchise is a door into the restaurant world. It is relatively safe, and you will be given lots of guidance and assistance by the franchisor. It may be that the guidance becomes more of a restriction than a support. You may feel that you could be making more profit if you did things differently. You may resent the fact that, of the profit you do make, a fair slice goes to the franchisor, and the more you make, the bigger the slice. If so, it could be time to move on and set up your own individual restaurant. However, you will not be able to capitalise on the success of the franchise outlet as the business is not yours to sell. The licence will include detailed terms for surrendering the franchise and, obviously, you will not be able to take the name and reputation with you. You will be able to capitalise on your experience, however, and this aspect of franchising is an excellent introduction to the restaurant business, and in itself can be financially rewarding.

The franchising contract

There is no specific legislation governing franchising, so the franchisor and franchisee relationship is governed by the contract of licence. It is usual for the franchisor to have a standard contract for all franchisees and, because of the powerful position of the franchisor, it is difficult for a franchisee to negotiate different terms. Nevertheless, it is important that all small print is scrutinised carefully and good legal advice obtained.

The wording of a franchising contract can also present financial drawbacks which are to be avoided. A franchisee makes two types of payment to the franchisor. There is the initial payment for the expertise, equipment and general know-how, and the second type of recurring payments (usually based on the gross takings), which is considered a management charge.

If the franchise contract is not specific about these payments, the Inland Revenue may treat the initial payment as of a capital nature and the management charges as royalties (in which case tax has to be deducted before payment is made to the franchisor). In the former case, a capital payment attracts only written-down allowances which, of course, is tax inefficient from the franchisee's point of view.

Assessing the franchise operation

There are a number of things to consider before signing the franchise agreement. First, one has to get to know the franchisor and the products. To get an insight into the franchisor's operation, visit the franchisor's offices and as many of the franchisees as possible. Scrutinise the franchise information pack and compare it with other competitors' information packs. It is also important to know the general background of the franchisor: how long it has been established, the financial performance over the past years, the number of outlets in the UK and worldwide.

To get a complete picture of the franchise operation, arrange to have informal meetings with other franchisees. The types of question to be covered include:

- What is the total start-up cost including any hidden costs, for example, additional contribution for equipment, uniforms?
- What contribution is required towards marketing and advertising costs?
- Is the franchisor's support reliable and how often do the franchisors send in their inspectors and auditors?
- Does the franchisor disagree over how the gross turnover, therefore the management fees, are worked out?
- What are the long-term prospects?
- Have all the equipment and stock provided been satisfactory?

You should also consider whether you personally would be happy working in that type of franchise. There are so many franchises available it should be easy to choose one that matches your aspirations in terms of the sort of restaurant you would like to run.

Some useful addresses

The British Franchise Association
Thames View, Newtown Road
Henley-on-Thames
Oxfordshire RG9 1HG
Tel. 0491 578049

The International Franchise Association
1025 Connecticut Avenue NW
Suite 1005
Washington DC 20036
USA

Chapter 5

Accountancy and Finance

Accounting and taxation

Often a restaurateur's first love is the food and his customers, but he must never lose sight of keeping proper management and control of the finances. This is very important because accurate, up-to-date accounts can help to monitor the performance of the restaurant, preventing cash flow catastrophes, as well as highlighting areas for improvement. Catering is a business where pennies count, and during recessionary times competition from other restaurants makes tight financial controls even more essential.

There is also the statutory requirement that proper accounting records are kept for Customs and Excise and the Inland Revenue. If your business is incorporated, you will probably have to file a set of accounts with Companies House in Cardiff. Even if you get your accountant to prepare the accounts, you remain responsible for the accuracy of the figures and the amount of the profits declared.

As the terminology and accounting principles used by the accounting profession can be complicated, this chapter will first examine VAT and then explain what, why and how the accounting records should be kept. It will make use of cash flow and monthly budget proformas.

VAT

Value added tax is a 17.5 per cent tax on all food and drinks sales for consumption on the premises of restaurants which have a taxable turnover of £45,000 or more in 12 months. The turnover limit for voluntary deregistration is £43,000. For take-away food, there is no VAT on cold food, and this includes cold drinks, bread, sandwiches, cold meats, pies and rolls. However, it must be pointed out that these zero-rated food and drinks have to be consumed away from the premises.

VAT is also payable on service charges though tips are not subject to VAT. Food and drink supplied to employees for which a charge is made is standard rated for VAT purposes but no tax is due if it is provided free. However, VAT is due on consumption by the proprietor and his family on certain items such as alcoholic drinks, soft drinks, ice-cream and confectionery.

How does VAT work?

VAT of 17.5 per cent has to be added to everything you sell (except cold take-away). In taxman's jargon, this is known as the *output tax*. At the same time you can claim back the VAT you pay on goods and services (with the exception of VAT on cars and entertainment). This is the *input tax*. There are a number of goods and services which are zero rated or exempt, that is, no VAT is charged on such items. These include raw foods, most insurance, postage etc. VAT is therefore not claimable from these payments. The rule of thumb for valid input tax is to ensure that your purchase invoices have a VAT registration number.

Every quarter you will receive a VAT return which you must complete promptly. Subtract your *input tax* from your *output tax* and pay the difference to Customs and Excise. If your input tax is greater than your output tax, you will receive a refund.

The VAT return must be submitted within a month of the end of each VAT quarter. It is important to file the VAT returns in time as Customs and Excise can impose penalties and interest on late payment.

You need to keep records of all the sales you make and VAT invoices from your suppliers as well as a summary of VAT for each quarter covered by your VAT returns. All business records should be kept for six years.

The 'hidden cost' of VAT

Too often many restaurants run into financial difficulties because of VAT due. You have to be aware of the hidden cost of VAT. It is generally accepted that the gross profit in the restaurant business is 45 per cent:

	£
Sales, ie food sold (net of VAT)	100
Cost of food goods	−55
Gross profit	45

The sale price is approximately twice the cost of food. So if the cost of a dish is £5, the sale price is not £10 but £11.75 (£1.75 has to be paid to Customs and Excise). Once you incorporate the cost of credit card charges (up to 5 per cent), you will realise that, unless the menu is priced with care, the profit margin can be small. To obtain a gross profit margin of £45, the sale price has to be £129.

	£
Gross sale price	129.00
VAT (17.5% of sale price)	−22.55
Credit card charges (5% of sale price)	−6.45
Cost of sales	−55.00
Gross profit	45.00

Always remember to build in the cost of VAT when pricing your menu.

Accounting records

The following accounting records need to be maintained:

- Cash payments book
- Cash receipts book
- Daily takings book
- Petty cash book
- Payroll records
- Unpaid purchase invoices.

Cash payments book

Date	Name of supplier	Cheque number	Gross amount	VAT	Purchases (food)	Beverage	Delivery charges	Wages and salaries
1.1.94	Dens Cash & Carry	100001	12315.12	57.75	12257.37			
3.1.94	Butter Gates & Co	100002	575.00	75.00				
3.1.94	Juffry Atun	100003	475.00					475.00
4.1.94	Annie	100004	375.00					375.00
5.1.94	Evergreen Printers	100005	125.00	18.62				
8.1.94	Sophia, Ahmed & Co	100006	235.00	35.00				
10.1.94	K D J Wines	100007	350.75	52.23		298.52		
12.1.94	Norbinsha Halal Butchers	100008	196.35		196.35			
12.1.94	IS & Co	100009	575.00	75.00				
16.1.94	Heppell & Starns garage	100010	322.98	48.10				
18.1.94	Dylan and Asoka Music	100011	35.58					
22.1.94	Stone Norwich Insurance	100012	780.00					
22.1.94	EJEA Supplies	100013	125.00				125.00	
25.1.94	AC & N Warehouse	100014	750.00	111.70		638.30		
27.1.94	British Telecom	100015	125.37	18.67				
29.1.94	TH A Consultancy	100016	900.00					
30.1.94	K C Sim	100017	350.00		350.00			
31.1.94	Drawings	100018	20000.00					20000.00
16.1.94	GE & H Insurance	direct debit	260.00					
15.1.94	Bank charges	direct debit	95.32					
20.1.94	Credit card charges	direct debit	1425.00					
			40391.47	492.07	12803.72	936.82	125.00	20850.00

Notes:
1. It is important that the VAT analysis is done properly. VAT is only claimable if you have an invoice which has the VAT registration number. Usually the VAT amount is shown separately. If this is not the case VAT is calculated as follows:

   Total from Evergreen Printers invoice shows £125.00
   VAT is therefore 17.5/117.5 × £125.00 = £18.61.

2. The direct debit items are obtained from the bank statements.
3. The VAT figure of £492.07 represents part of the VAT output for January 1994.

Cash payments book

This book records all the payments you make by cheque as well as all the standing orders, direct debits, bank charges and other items deducted from your bank account. These items are obtained from the bank statements which you should retain and file neatly. Make a habit of writing up your cashbook as often as possible and certainly not less frequently than once a month. Your cash payments book should have at least 16 columns.

You will need to keep a separate cash book for each current account you hold.

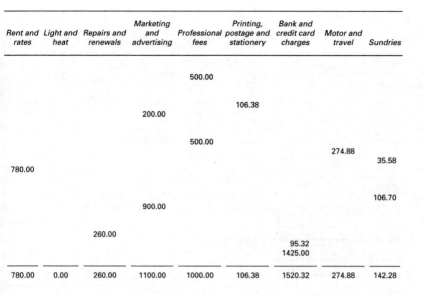

Rent and rates	Light and heat	Repairs and renewals	Marketing and advertising	Professional fees	Printing, postage and stationery	Bank and credit card charges	Motor and travel	Sundries
				500.00				
					106.38			
			200.00					
				500.00				
							274.88	
								35.58
780.00								
								106.70
			900.00					
		260.00						
						95.32		
						1425.00		
780.00	0.00	260.00	1100.00	1000.00	106.38	1520.32	274.88	142.28

Cash receipts book

The cash receipts book records the monies received either from the restaurant takings or other deposits (for example, capital introduced).

A five- or six-column cash book should be used and should also be written up as frequently as possible.

Cash receipts book

Date	Total	Cash	Cheques	Daily sales takings Credit cards	American Express	Other
1.1.94	1279.00	0.00	75.35	1203.65		
2.1.94	1504.60	250.00	25.10	1194.50		35.00
3.1.94	899.80	0.00	210.00	689.80		
4.1.94	995.56	75.00	35.74	798.92	85.90	
5.1.94	675.14	0.00	22.39	652.75		
6.1.94	566.37	0.00	21.56	544.81		
7.1.94	949.27	0.00	120.00	829.27		
etc						
31.1.94	1909.62	0.00	52.37	1857.25		
Total	39817.31	850.00	3552.24	33382.57	1957.50	75.00

Notes:
1. The cash column shows the amount of cash banked, not the actual takings.
2. The items in the Total column should agree with the entries on the bank statements.

Daily takings book (page 45)

This records the daily takings and is used as the basis for the calculations of VAT output. It should ideally be written up daily but certainly not less than once a week.

Petty cash book (page 46)

This is an important accounting book to maintain accurately because of the cash transactions of the catering trade. There are a lot of these; for example, when buying from butchers, fishmongers and some of the staff costs. It is unlikely that all the cash received will be banked as many of the payments and purchases have to be settled in cash. All the cash not banked has to be entered in the receipt side. All the payments made by cash have to be recorded, and all the invoices/documentation must be retained. The petty cash book is columnar, and again it is important to analyse the VAT correctly.

Payroll records

As it is common for restaurants to employ casual labour, a casual wages register must be kept for each individual employed. The following details have to be kept:

1. Name
2. Address
3. Amount earned
4. Amount of tax deducted.

Daily takings book

Date	Total £	Cash	Cheque	Credit cards	American Express	Other	Analysis (includes VAT) Food	Drinks	Service charge (10%)
1.1.94	1550.75	221.50	75.35	1203.65	50.25	35.00	1057.79	352.00	140.96
2.1.94	1675.95	421.35	25.10	1194.50			1278.61	245.00	152.34
3.1.94	990.00	90.20	210.00	689.80			804.26	95.75	89.99
4.1.94	987.36	122.25	35.74	798.92	30.45		777.61	120.00	89.75
5.1.94	1025.34	350.20	22.39	652.75			796.39	135.75	93.20
6.1.94	1112.37	221.00	21.56	544.81	325.00		789.06	222.20	101.11
7.1.94	1001.58	52.31	120.00	829.27			815.54	95.00	91.04
etc									
31.1.94	1952.12	42.50	52.37	1857.25			1499.67	275.00	177.45
Total	45230.21	6820.10	3552.24	33382.57	2200.30	75.00	33527.79	7590.99	4111.43

45230.21

Notes:
1. The total column is the daily gross takings, including VAT, tips and service charge.
2. The need to differentiate American Express receipts is because Amex will remit to you net of their charges, while Visa and Mastercard will pay you the gross amount and deduct their total charges by direct debit monthly from your bank account. By having different columns, it will be easier for you to check that the correct amounts have been received.
3. The daily takings need to be analysed into food sales, drinks and service charges.

Petty cash book

Date	Receipts				Payments				
	Cash sales	Others	Total	Total	VAT	Wages	Food	Drinks	Sundries
1.1.94		150.00		135.75	1.20	120.00	0.00	0.00	14.55
2.1.94	221.50	250.00		95.84	7.50	15.00	58.34	15.00	0.00
3.1.94	171.35			225.75	15.74	0.00	25.01	170.00	15.00
4.1.94	90.20			0.00	0.00	0.00	0.00	0.00	0.00
5.1.94	47.25			5.65	0.00	0.00	0.00	0.00	5.65
etc									
31.1.94	42.50			75.25	1.35	0.00	61.90	0.00	12.00
	5970.10	3000.00	8970.10	8875.90	136.65	4500.00	1084.93	2500.00	654.32

Reconciliation

Balance brought forward from 31.12.93	125.35
Payments	−8875.90
Receipts	8970.10
Balance carried forward to 1.2.94	219.55

Notes:

1. *Cash sales* receipts represent the difference between the actual cash sales taking and the amount of cash banked.
2. *Others* include monies withdrawn from the bank as well as capital introduced by the proprietor.
3. A monthly reconciliation needs to be done. The balance carried forward tells you how much you should have in your petty cash box at that date.

Payroll records

Week ending _____

Name	(a) Basic pay in the week	(b) Overtime	(c) Tips	(d) Total pay (a+b+c)	(e) Tax due	(f) Employee's NIC	(g) Other deductions	(h) Net pay (d-e-f-g)	(i) Employer's NIC

Notes:
1. The total wage for the week includes overtime, tips and service charges.
2. The National Insurance contributions figures are obtained from the NIC tables provided by the Inland Revenue.
3. The tax due will depend on the employee's tax coding and earnings to date.
4. The Other deductions column is for miscellaneous items; for instance, the repayment of an advance.

Service charges paid by customers and passed on direct to the employee by the restaurant are also subject to Pay As You Earn (PAYE) through the payroll.

As an employer you are responsible for deducting income tax and National Insurance contributions (NIC) under PAYE as well as paying employer's NIC to the Inland Revenue. You should get an IR5 leaflet and a New Employer's Starter Pack from your local tax office as these will contain all the instructions and forms you will need.

If you find working out PAYE too difficult or time-consuming, there are many payroll bureaux which will do the job for you. Either use the form provided by the Inland Revenue or develop your own payroll records along the lines of the proforma shown on page 47.

Unpaid purchase invoices

As it is normal for trade suppliers to give settlement credit, it is important that unpaid invoices are kept and filed properly. It is good practice to keep these purchase invoices in a separate file or folder in either alphabetical or date order. As the payment is made, remove the invoice from the folder and file it with other paid invoices. To avoid duplicating payment, either cross the invoice or write 'paid' on the invoice, and the date when paid. If you paid by cheque, it is good practice to note down the cheque number.

Cash flow management

A large number of profitable businesses collapse simply because of poor cash flow management. Cash flow problems arise when there is insufficient money in the bank to meet the daily running bills of the business. This may be caused by customers being slow to pay.

For the restaurant business, where customers are expected to pay as soon as they finish eating, cash flow problems usually arise when the proprietor does not put sufficient money aside for certain large bills which have accrued; for instance, last quarter's VAT or the council rates.

Proper cash flow management can help to forecast future

cash requirements as well as identify any problems which may arise.

Preparing a cash flow statement

Cash flow statements will need to have two columns for each month – forecast and actual figures. You will need to prepare a cash flow forecast prior to commencing trading (see business plan on page 31). At the end of each month of trading, you will have to insert the actual payments made and deduct the total expenses from total income and add to the bank balance brought forward to tell how much you have. Comparison with the actual figures will assist in pinpointing areas where cost has to be reduced.

Operating budget

Many proprietors do not know how much profit or loss is made until the accounts have been prepared by the accountant, which could be many months after the end of the financial period.

An operating budget helps you to forecast your profit or loss and enables you to compare your projections with actual performances.

Cash flow statement for the year ending 31.12.1995

	Pre-trading		January	
	Forecast	Actual	Forecast	Actual
INCOME				
Cash sales				
Cheques and credit cards				
American Express				
Capital introduced				
Bank loans				
Interest and other income				
(A) TOTAL £				
EXPENDITURE				
Cash purchases				
Credit purchases				
Drinks and alcohol				
Wages and salaries				
Delivery charges				
Inland Revenue				
Rent and rates				
Light and heat				
Repairs and renewals				
Marketing and advertising				
Legal fees				
Audit and accountancy				
Bank interest				
Bank charges				
Loan interest				
Motor and travel				
Drawings				
Credit card charges				
Printing, postage and stationery				
Sundries				
Capital expenditure				
VAT				
(B) TOTAL £				
Cash inflow/outflow (A–B)				
Opening balance (C)				
Closing balance (C)+(A–B)				

February		March etc		......	Total (for year)	
Forecast	*Actual*	*Forecast*	*Actual*		*Forecast*	*Actual*

———	———	———	———		———	———
———	———	———	———		———	———
———	———	———	———		———	———
———	———	———	———		———	———
———	———	———	———		———	———
———	———	———	———		———	———

Operating budget for the year to 31.12.95

	January		February	
	Forecast	Actual	Forecast	Actual

SALES (less VAT)

Food
Alcoholic beverages
Take-away
Others

      TOTAL SALES (A)

LESS COST OF SALES (B)

Purchase of food
Purchase of alcoholic drinks
Delivery charges

(C) GROSS PROFIT (A)–(B)

(D) GROSS PROFIT AS A
PERCENTAGE OF SALES

$(C)/(A) \times 100 = (D)$

LESS ADMINISTRATION

Wages and salaries
Proprietor's drawings
Rent
Rates
Light and heat
Repairs and renewals
Marketing and advertising
Legal fees
Audit and accountancy
Motor and travel
Printing, postage and stationery
Sundries

DEPRECIATION

FINANCE CHARGES

Bank interest
Bank charges
Loan interest
Credit card charges

(E) TOTAL OVERHEADS

(F) NET PROFIT BEFORE TAX
    (C)–(E)

(F) SALES TO BREAK EVEN
    $(E)/(D) \times 100$

	March etc		...	Total (for year)	
Forecast	*Actual*			*Forecast*	*Actual*

Chapter 6

Advertising and Marketing

Marketing is essential to ensure the success of your restaurant. You must not assume that customers will visit your restaurant simply because it is there or continue to do so just because you have served them one good meal. People visit restaurants for many reasons and eating is just one of them. You have to create a positive image and an awareness of who you are and what type of food you have on your menu. Though there is no doubt that a restaurant can succeed on its reputation, you must still advertise actively, especially in recessionary times. You have to increase interest for passers-by to come into your restaurant and, more importantly, you need to encourage consumers' confidence in your food and service. As a restaurateur, you have to convince prospective and regular customers to eat in your restaurant, whether to celebrate a special occasion, as a meeting place with friends and business colleagues, to save having to cook at home or to eat something different from the food usually cooked at home. Customers will patronise your restaurant for these reasons if they know they will get a satisfying 'meal experience' from your restaurant.

The 'meal experience'

The meal experience includes all the actions and feelings involved in coming to your restaurant. This will start from first stepping into your restaurant, enjoying the atmosphere, good service and food, to finally leaving the restaurant. Before looking into the factors which constitute an enjoyable meal experience, you must first consider the marketing strategies in order to attract customers to visit your restaurant for the 'meal experience'. What are the reasons for going out for a meal and the factors which help the customers to decide where they like to have their 'meal experience'? Many people eat out to celebrate special occasions such as St Valentine's day, an anniversary, Christmas, a birthday etc. Therefore, make sure that your restaurant gives the impression that these special occasions should be celebrated there. For instance, ensure that your restaurant is decorated to suit events like St Valentine's day or Christmas. Have special menus to celebrate those occasions. Offer complimentary drinks for birthday celebrations. Other main reasons why people eat out are to save having to cook, casual meetings with friends, treating a spouse or relatives, and to experiment with the type of food offered. All these will depend on the type of restaurant you have. If you want to run an up-market restaurant, you will not want customers coming in wearing casual clothing just for a quick meal. If, on the other hand, you run a middle-of-the-market restaurant, you will want to create a relaxed atmosphere after a hectic day's work as well as suit customers having a business meal. Much of this will depend on the image the restaurant itself portrays. For example, the attire of the staff, the decorations of the premises and, most important, the price and type of menu.

Factors which can improve the meal experience include the following:

- Creating a positive image
- Service
- General atmosphere
- Quality of food served.

Creating a positive image
The public image of your restaurant is important. The exterior appearance of the restaurant has to be attractive in order to encourage customers to enter. Make sure that the area around the restaurant is kept clean, the windows polished and that the menu displayed is appealing, clear and well lit. When the customers step into the restaurant, greet them warmly, and show them promptly to their table.

Service from the staff
One of the most important aspects of any meal experience is

the service from the waiters and waitresses. Good service can enhance the taste of the meal as well as attract the customers to return. Bad service is a certain turn-off; even with the best food, customers are very unlikely to return.

The waiters and waitresses have to be well trained. They must be presentable, polite and appropriately dressed. All the waiting staff must know the menu thoroughly in order to be able to recommend dishes and drinks. They have to be alert and quick to respond when service is required.

Give the customers the feeling of personalisation. Have friendly conversations and make every effort to remember the names of regular customers.

General atmosphere

The customers' meal experience will depend on the general atmosphere of the restaurant. This is affected by the decorations and interior design, the sound levels, the type of background music being played, the overall cleanliness of the establishment, the bar area and lavatories, the other customers and the service from the staff. It is important to ensure that there is harmony so that customers can eat and feel completely relaxed. The personality of the restaurateur can also help here, and you as the owner must get to know your regular customers. Customers generally appear to enjoy going more often to a restaurant where they know the owner. A customer who feels valued will identify with the restaurant and will think of it as his or her own special place or 'find'.

Serving food

The most important aspect of a meal experience is the food. Therefore, the type of menu offered and the variety of choice will have to be planned thoroughly.

Moreover, there must be consistency in the quality and quantity of the food served, to meet the expectations of regular customers. This is sometimes difficult to maintain if you have changed chefs or when the main chef is off duty. Also, the kitchen staff must be well trained as they are the people who will be preparing the food.

Another important factor is the wine list. Make sure that you have stocked all the wines and other alcoholic drinks listed, and that the drinks are served at the correct temperature. Try to recommend wines for particular dishes as you have to give the impression that the wines on the list have been specially selected to accompany the dishes on your menu.

Marketing your restaurant

Even if your restaurant has the right recipe for customers to have a pleasant 'meal experience', you must still actively sell the restaurant and your products. This is especially relevant in recessionary times when eating out is not as common as it was in the roaring 1980s.

Therefore, you will need to find out about your customers, especially how adventurous they are in trying new recipes, and how much they are willing to pay. Ideally, you will want to charge as much as possible, but at the same time you want the customers to feel that they have had a value-for-money meal. Sales promotion can be used to market a new item on the menu, either by recommending it to the customers or by having a prominent sign offering the promotion.

Another way of successfully marketing your restaurant is to look at weekly and monthly sales trends. There are certain times of the week and certain months of the year when there are bound to be slack sales. This is when you must have special promotions and other sales gimmicks as well as advertise. Normally, the early part of the week is quieter. It is worth considering having special promotions on Mondays to Thursdays, such as a complimentary glass of house wine with the meal. Also, customers always like to eat at the same time, usually after eight. Many restaurants try to spread the flow of the customers by encouraging them to turn up earlier by having happy hours in the early evening. There are certain months of the year when the restaurant trade will be miserable. January is usually the worst month in the year as customers are recovering from Christmas; July and August can also be dreadful as people go away on holiday. This is not obviously the case if your restaurant is in a holiday resort or is in an area frequented by holiday makers from abroad. Nevertheless, you will need to find out the quiet months for your restaurant and have sales promotions and increase your advertising in these months.

Sales promotion

Sales promotion is a good marketing tool to encourage people to spend more. Sales promotion comes in many forms. A restaurant may offer a 10 per cent discount on all meals in January or a free bottle of wine for two set dinners ordered during an off-peak period. Another good sales promotion is to be a loss leader in a common product which all other restaurants sell; for example, selling your bottle of house wine considerably cheaper than all your competitors. If your bottle of wine is £2 cheaper than can be obtained in another nearby restaurant, the customer will get the impression that the price of your food is also considerably cheaper.

Advertising

Before deciding on the form of advertising, you need to know the amount of money budgeted for it. You will then need to consider how to target the type of people who will visit your restaurant. A successful advertising campaign should influence the target customers' attitudes and behaviour in such a way as to make them want to visit your restaurant. Therefore, you will need to advertise in the media which are most likely to reach them. One of the most popular forms of advertising for restaurants is the local newspaper because it is much cheaper and will reach a larger proportion of target customers.

What type of ad?

A restaurant must have a distinctive logo which should be compatible with the theme of the establishment. A good advertisement must be eye-catching and effective, and get right to the point with a simple but powerful message.

Tell people why they should visit your restaurant in preference to a competitor's: 'home cooking with only the freshest spices' or 'best value for money'. In other words, use phrases and ideas that have a positive connotation which will persuade people to try your restaurant. However, remember that you have to be honest and do not claim to be something which you are not. This will not only put customers off but you are also likely to be prosecuted (see Chapter 9). Though most local newspapers have advertising and marketing staff who will help you with the design and logo, it may be worthwhile asking a creative local artist to do the work. It is not advisable to ask an advertising agency as this is likely to be too expensive.

Kinds of advertisement

When you advertise a special sales promotion, be aware of what your competitors are doing. You do not want to promote the sale of your bottle of house wine at £6.95, saying it is the cheapest in town, when a nearby restaurant is selling its bottle for only £5.95. The loss leader advertising technique is generally used to stimulate sales in the quiet months or to get new customers. During recessionary times, many restaurants have an 'eat as much as you like' offer. Though this may certainly prompt interest, such offers are only likely to succeed in large restaurant chains. Such sale gimmicks may also give your restaurant a bad image as well as attract customers who are unlikely to spend much at other times.

How to advertise

Press advertising

Newspapers. Local newspapers are the most popular way to advertise. As the advertisement is likely to be in the 'Eating Out' section, your advertisement must stand out from the rest. If you advertise in several local papers, you should keep records of all the advertisements in order to know which has been most effective. A highly recommended and effective advertisement is to offer customers a certain percentage discount if they present the ad and use it within a certain period. This will not only give you an idea of which local papers are most effective, but also help to stimulate sales in the quieter periods.

Guides. Try to get your restaurant in one of the 'good food guides', eg *The Egon Ronay Guide, The AA Guide* or *Time Out* because they have large circulations and are bought by people who are most likely to eat out. You will need to contact the publishers directly and, after some formal visits, your restaurant may be included. Whenever there is a write-up in the press, always take a cutting (enlarge it if necessary) and put it in the window. You will be surprised how these write-ups can attract prospective customers. This is, of course, assuming that the restaurant has had a good write-up.

Signs

To be effective, signs should draw people's immediate attention. They have to be clear and simple, and the primary focus of a restaurant sign should be limited to the name and type of restaurant. It should be positioned close to the restaurant. Such signs are more appropriate for restaurants dependent on passing trade. An up-market restaurant in a residential area will not need such a sign.

Direct mail and door-to-door leaflet drops

A leaflet drop is one of the most effective ways of communicating directly with targeted customers. The cheapest method is to ask someone to distribute the leaflets in specific defined areas rather than post through the mail. This is one of the most cost-effective methods of advertising and the feedback from targeted customers is easy to appraise. The main advantage of direct mail is that specific customers can be targeted, and a personal message included. Regular customers can be reminded of the restaurant with Christmas cards, details of special promotions and other special offers. The leaflets and literature must be of good quality and eye-catching. It is also a good idea to include the whole menu in the leaflet. Sales promotion in quieter periods can also make use of this type of advertising.

Television and radio

These are only appropriate if you run a whole chain of restaurants nationally, as they are very costly. Even broadcasting on the local radio station is probably not value for money because a 15-second radio spot can only be heard at the time it is aired, while a local newspaper can be picked up and read at any time, and kept for future reference.

Public relations

This involves the creation of a favourable social environment in the well-defined community in which the restaurant operates. It includes getting along with local businesses as well as being friendly with nearby pub landlords, as they can recommend new customers. A restaurateur must also develop good relationships with officials. When you first move into your premises, contact the local council about the regulations relating to health and safety as well as Food Safety Acts (Chapter 9). If there is anything you are not certain of, the local council can be a tremendous help. More importantly, you have to build up goodwill with the local police, and it is always advisable to make the first move and introduce yourself at the local police station. You will certainly require their assistance one way or another later on.

Chapter 7
Professional Advisers

It is inevitable that you will need a range of professional advisers, both when you plan to start up your restaurant and when it is up and running. For example, you will need an accountant, a lawyer, perhaps a surveyor etc. These services do not come cheaply, but a good adviser's help is invaluable. Make sure that you make the best use of your advisers, monitor their fees carefully and be prepared to negotiate hard and shop around.

Who are these professional advisers?

- Accountant/tax adviser/auditor
- Architect/interior designer
- Bank manager
- Catering consultant and catering organisations
- Estate agent/surveyor
- Government bodies
- Insurance broker
- Solicitor.

Where to find them?

- Word of mouth, especially from colleagues in the catering trade. This is probably the most reliable source of information about the quality of an adviser
- List of local professional advisers from Enterprise Agencies
- Recommendations from your bank manager or other professional person
- Advertisements in the local and national press
- Yellow Pages and Thomson Directories

● Respective professional bodies' list of members' publications obtainable in most libraries.

How much do they cost?

This will depend on the time spent by the adviser on your work. Always ask for a fee quotation. You will be surprised how much the charges can vary if you shop around. Beware of professional 'dirty tricks' especially during a recession. Sometimes professional advisers quote low fees initially to attract your business. This is particularly true of accountants at the moment. By all means accept a low-fee quotation but do be aware that the accountant may try to add extra costs to subsequent work, such as taxation advice. For example, it is customary to retain the same accountant for future years. You may be dismayed to see how your accountancy and audit fees begin to rise. Although this technique has been widely criticised, and condemned by professional ethics bodies, it is still common.

To use professional advisers fully, you must have a clear idea what is expected of them. Always be aware of the respective profession's code of practice by which members of the profession are obliged to abide. In a professional relationship, in addition to any contractual duty, there is also a duty of care.

It is important to cultivate a serious-minded relationship with your advisers. Good advice can be the difference between success and failure. You are entitled to expect a high standard of work from a professional adviser, and should insist on their putting right any short-comings in their work. If they continue not to perform satisfactorily, change your adviser.

Accountants

A good firm of accountants can be of immense help because they can advise on the setting-up of the business (eg sole trader, partnership or limited company and, very importantly, tax planning), as well as ensure that the business complies with the law (eg that the accounting and payroll records are properly maintained). Accountants can also help in raising finance with the banks, particularly with the preparation of your business plan's financial projections. When you set up initially, it is unlikely that you will need to employ a full-time accountant.

Even if you do not engage an accountant when you first set up, you will eventually need to have one to draw up the annual accounts as well as an annual audit (if you have a limited company). Most important of all, a good accountant can help to minimise business tax as well as agree tax assessments with the Inland Revenue.

The Institute of Chartered Accountants publishes an annual directory of firms which contains detailed information about individual practices.

Architects and chartered surveyors

If you plan to renovate or rebuild part of your premises, you will need to employ architects and chartered surveyors to design and draw plans for local planning permission applications. Depending on the amount of designing and alteration work needed, it is sometimes more appropriate to have an architect and not a chartered surveyor, and vice versa. You must ensure that the surveyor is a member of a professional association such as the Royal Institution of Chartered Surveyors (RICS) or the Incorporated Society of Valuers and Auctioneers (ISVA). You can obtain a detailed list of architectural firms from the RIBA (Royal Institute of British Architects) Directory of Practices.

Bank managers

Bank managers, who once upon a time were the champions of small business, have become the Scrooge of many new businesses. Owing to the large number of business failures in the early 1990s, the banks are now unwilling to assist new businesses unless the proprietor is willing to put up a large proportion of the capital.

Catering consultants and organisations

A list of catering consultants is obtainable from the Hotel, Catering and Institutional Management Association (HCIMA), 191 Trinity Road, London SW17 7HN; 081-672 4251.

Other useful organisations include the British Hotels Association, based at 40 Duke Street, London W1M 5DA; 071-499 6641; and the Hotel and Catering Training Company, International House, High Street, London W5 5DB; 081-579 2400.

Estate agents

You may need estate agents in the preliminary stages while looking for premises. There is normally no charge for their services and commissions are payable by the vendors. Estate agents have to comply with the Estate Agents Act 1979, which is policed by the Office of Fair Trading.

Government bodies

Though one does not usually consider government bodies in the same category as other professional advisers, you must not underestimate the usefulness of the many departments; for instance, Local Enterprise Agencies, Training and Enterprise Councils (TECs) in England and Wales and Local Enterprise Companies (LECs) in Scotland. They provide excellent business advice which is normally free. You can find your nearest Local Enterprise Agency by contacting: Business in the Community (BIC), 8 Stratton Street, London W1X 5FD; 071-629 1600.

You can get in touch with your local TEC by writing to: Business and Enterprise Branch, Employment Department, Room N807, Moorfoot, Sheffield S1 4PQ.

Insurance brokers

You will need many different insurance covers for your restaurant business. It is advisable to find a reliable insurance broker to arrange all your requirements.

- Building and contents insurance
- Employer's liability
- Public liability as well as third party public liability insurance
- Insurance of stock
- Motor insurance
- Permanent health insurance
- Keyman insurance.

Solicitors

The engagement of a solicitor is unavoidable. You need one at the preliminary stages with the purchase of the premises or the lease agreements. A good solicitor will also help in ensuring that the contracts are drawn up to your benefit.

Your solicitor will handle all the legal formalities of the formation of the restaurant including drawing up contracts of employment. You will also need him or her to apply for the grant of a licence for the restaurant.

You will find a list of local solicitors in the Regional Directory of Solicitors or from the Secretary of the local Law Society. It is, however, advisable to engage a solicitor by personal recommendation.

Chapter 8

Personnel Management

There are two main aspects of personnel management. First, there are the complex and ever-changing employment laws and statutory requirements that all restaurateurs have to be aware of, and, second, the important job of recruiting good chefs and waiting staff, motivating and retaining them. Good personnel management is vital for the success of any restaurant. A pleasurable meal experience (see Chapter 6) will depend on the calibre and dedication of your staff.

Employment law covers wages, dismissals, health and safety at work, discrimination and trade union rules. As an employer, you also need to know the legislation governing recruitment of staff, employment contracts and statutory rights of employees.

As a restaurateur, you have to be aware of the legal requirements of both the Sex Discrimination Act 1975 and the Race Relations Act 1976. Your advertisements must not be discriminative; for example, do not use terms such as 'waitress' (instead refer to waiters and waitresses as waiting staff) or 'black person'. However, if you run an ethnic restaurant, for example, an Indian restaurant, it is acceptable to advertise for an Indian waiter, as such a person is necessary for authentic cuisine.

You must also try not to mention an age band for the job advertised. For example, a female applicant can claim sexual discrimination if an age restriction of 25 to 35 for women is specified. She could claim that the employer is choosing women on the basis of their appearance, whereas a man would not be subjected to this test.

Employment law

Terms of the contract of employment

Under the Employment Protection (Consolidation) Act 1978, the employer must give each employee a written statement setting out the terms and conditions of employment if the employee is going to work for more than 16 hours per week. An additional note on disciplinary and grievance procedures must also be included.

These are some of the important points to be included in the contract:

- The rate of pay and whether it is to be paid weekly or monthly
- Date of commencement of employment
- Job title and the location
- The normal hours of work and terms and conditions relating to overtime
- Holidays and holiday pay
- Provision for sick pay
- Pension schemes (if applicable)
- Notice of termination of employment required by both parties
- Disciplinary rules relating to the job and grievance procedure.

Disciplinary practice and procedures

Disciplinary procedures should be designed to encourage improvements in the employees' conduct, and not as a means of imposing restrictions and sanctions.

Disciplinary procedures should therefore:

- specify to whom they apply
- specify the procedure to be followed
- provide for matters to be dealt with
- indicate the disciplinary actions to be taken
- specify the person who has the authority to dismiss
- ensure that no employee is dismissed for the first breach of discipline except for gross misconduct

- ensure that disciplinary action is not taken until the case has been carefully investigated
- provide a right of appeal.

Wages and salaries

You are required to issue a payslip with the pay cheque or cash payment as well as an itemised statement detailing gross salary, net salary, deductions made (National Insurance, PAYE) and details of part payments (eg overtime).

Statutory rights of employees

An employee is protected by many statutory rules and regulations, whereas a casual labourer has few rights. Whether your staff are employees or casuals will depend on various factors such as how much control you have over them, whether you provide the equipment or they provide their own, whether they are obliged to work a specified number of hours a week.

Most staff will qualify as employees, although in certain circumstances you may employ people as casual workers. A typical casual worker is not expected to have regular work, but is instead called upon occasionally when the need arises. For example, extra waiting staff may be called in to staff an unusually large event.

Always seek the advice of your solicitor when employing staff. It is worth drawing up a proper contract of employment, and that the staff member's status as an employee or casual worker is clear to both parties. This should avoid legal disputes in the future. Your solicitor will also advise you on how to comply with employment legislation. The main areas are the Employment (Consolidation) Act 1978, the Health and Safety at Work Act 1974, and laws concerning race and sex discrimination.

A summary of the statutory rights
On commencement of employment, an employee has the right:

– not to be unlawfully discriminated against on the grounds of sex, race or marital status;

- to receive a statement of terms and conditions of employment within eight weeks as well as an itemised pay statement;
- to take time off for trade union activities;
- not to have unlawful deductions from salary;
- to have access to computer data held on him or her;
- to seek compensation for damages caused by the unauthorised or inaccurate disclosure of data.

After a month of working the employee has the right:

- to receive a guarantee payment for up to five days if you are unable to provide work in any three-month period;
- to receive up to 26 weeks' pay if suspended on medical grounds;
- to one week's paid notice if you should decide to terminate employment.

After six months, the employee has the right to receive a written statement on dismissal.

After two years (or five years for employees who work less than 16 hours but more than eight hours per week), the employee has the right:

- to receive maternity pay and to return to work;
- not to be unfairly dismissed;
- to statutory redundancy payment if the requirement for the employee's work ceases;
- to one week's paid notice for each full year of employment, to a maximum of 12 weeks.

Other legal aspects
You are vicariously liable for the actions of your employees taken during the course of their employment. Therefore, if an outbreak of food poisoning arises from your chef's cooking, you become vicariously liable.

The employee is obliged to obey reasonable orders and instructions from the employer. The employee also owes you a duty of fidelity, ie a duty of confidence regarding the restaurant's trade secrets as well as to use skill and care in his or her work.

Right of employees to take time off

Other than bank holidays, the employee has to negotiate all other holidays with you. The European Community recommends four weeks' paid leave a year.

There are, however, statutory rights to have time off in a number of situations, including jury service and trade union activities.

Statutory requirements of Income Tax (Employments) Regulations 1973

You must not underestimate the importance of this legislation as the Inland Revenue have been given considerable powers to access all your records and information. They have ways of detecting fraud and neglect. The Inland Revenue can also impose stiff financial penalties as well as criminal prosecutions.

The PAYE system

The Inland Revenue will send you a New Employer's Starter Pack, which is comprehensive and easily understood. The PAYE system requires the employer to deduct tax at source from salaries and account for it and National Insurance contributions to the Inland Revenue. The tax to be deducted under PAYE will depend on the employee's tax code. This is provided by the Inland Revenue. The Inland Revenue also provide the tables for the computation of tax and National Insurance contributions.

As soon as the restaurant commences trading, you must inform your local tax office, which will then assign you a PAYE tax reference number. They will also provide you with a number and the name of a person whom you can contact if there is any query.

Administration

When a new employee arrives, a form P45 (which the employee is given by his previous employers) should be produced from which details can be entered on a deductions working sheet. If the employee is unable to supply a P45, you have to fill in form P46 (a substitute for P45). The P46 has to be submitted to the Tax Office.

When an employee leaves, a P45 has to be completed showing the tax code, pay and tax deducted up to the date of leaving.

Tax and National Insurance contributions have to be paid to the Inland Revenue within 14 days of the end of each month. There is, however, special provision for quarterly accounting provided the total is below a certain threshold.

At the end of each year (the tax year ends on 5 April), you have to submit to the Inland Revenue a number of forms:

- End of year returns (P14): Summary for each employee showing total pay, tax, National Insurance contributions, Statutory Sick pay (SSP) and Statutory Maternity Pay (SMP).
- End of year summary (P35): Details of all the end of year returns.
- P11D: For employees earning more than £8500, information on expenses and benefits.

The P14s and P35s have to be submitted by 19 May and P11Ds by 6 May.

Each employee must also be given a form P60 at the end of the financial year. This shows the total pay and tax, National Insurance number, tax code, and the employee's name and address.

If you find the administration of PAYE too time-consuming and tedious, ask your accountant to do it. There are also many payroll bureaux which can do all your payroll administration for less than what your accountant will charge.

Recruiting staff

When recruiting staff, much time and effort must be spent on ensuring that only the best staff are selected. The chef must obviously be able to cook to the standard and quality you require and a good chef is one of the most important assets of a restaurant. Customers will return if they enjoy the meal, so do spend time searching and be prepared to pay well to retain your chef – it is common for good chefs to be poached by competitors!

Try not to be too dependent on one chef. It has been known for some restaurants to close down when the main chef has left. To safeguard yourself, it is advisable to have an assistant chef who is able to take over the chef's job at short notice, as well as cover for the main chef on his nights off.

Although waiters and waitresses are easier to replace than chefs, due care and attention must be given to their recruitment. Your restaurant needs efficient staff who are alert, quick on their toes, with a professional attitude. Good service from your waiting staff will certainly enhance the meal experience of the customers.

Poor service can be a complete turn-off for customers. It is unlikely that they will return to a restaurant with unfriendly and rude staff, no matter how good the food may be.

Kitchen staff must be willing to obey instructions and learn quickly so that the kitchen is run smoothly and efficiently. The staff must be properly trained as most kitchen accidents are due to human error.

Owner and employee relations

Good communication
When the restaurant is busy, orders must be obeyed and it is important that staff can trust each other and not bear grudges. There must always be good communication and mutual respect between the restaurateur and his staff. When it is necessary to reprimand an employee it is good practice to do so privately rather than in front of other staff or customers. You also need to be careful with your choice of words. This is especially true if you employ staff from foreign nationalities and cultures, as they may have different codes of conduct.

Motivation and staff morale
Waiters and waitresses are usually motivated to work hard to keep the customers satisfied because gratuities left by customers will depend largely on the service received. It is, however, not so simple to motivate kitchen staff. Therefore,

it is really up to you to maintain the morale of all your employees. An environment which is pleasant to work in will help. Many restaurants have special incentive schemes where all the employees receive a bonus if specific sales targets are reached. Compliments should also be paid when due.

Setting restaurant policies

You need to have a set of policies for all staff, such as no smoking while at work. The other important restaurant guideline is the employee food policy. It is up to you whether you implement an 'eat as much as you like' policy or charge a certain percentage of the menu price. Do bear in mind that it is tempting for staff to abuse privileges given, so it is advisable to have a policy with clear limits. A good policy is to give a free meal but limit the choice to meals which are not too expensive or difficult to prepare.

Chapter 9
The Law and the Restaurateur

A restaurant has to comply with many rules and regulations. Although you may at first be overwhelmed by their sheer number, they are based on common sense and exist to protect the health and safety of the customers and restaurant staff. Your solicitor will help you to ensure that you fulfil your legal requirements which cover the following topics:

- Statutory requirements of the Inland Revenue and HM Customs and Excise (see Chapter 8)
- Licensing laws
- Food safety and hygiene
- Consumer legislation
- Health and safety at work
- Employment law (see Chapter 8)
- Employment of children
- Music and the law.

Licensing laws

There are two types of licence which a restaurateur can apply for: a restaurant licence or an ordinary justices' licence with a condition that a drink may be served only with a meal.

It is advisable to apply for the restaurant licence because it is more readily granted than a justices' licence. A restaurant licence can only be rejected on very limited grounds such as the applicant is under 21 years old or the premises will not be used to provide proper meals.

The procedures to be followed when making a licence application are covered in Chapter 2. There are two conditions attached to a restaurant licence:

1. Alcohol can be served only to customers taking table

meals. Alcohol must not be sold for take-away meals.
2. The restaurant must be able to serve soft drinks as well as alcohol.

Currently the permitted hours to sell alcohol are:

– On weekdays other than Christmas Day or Good Friday, 11.00 am–11.00 pm.
– On Sundays, Christmas Day and Good Friday, 12.00 pm–3.00 pm and 7.00 pm–10.30 pm.

An extended hours order may be applied for and this will extend the permitted hours for a further hour on weekdays (except Good Friday and Maundy Thursday). The making of an extended hours order is discretionary and anyone may object to an application for such an order.

Where live music and dancing or the service of substantial refreshment are provided, a restaurant can apply for a *special hours certificate*. This will extend licensing hours to 2.00 am on weekdays (other than Good Friday and Maundy Thursday), and on any day when there is no music and dancing after 12.00, the permitted hours end at midnight.

It is an offence to serve alcohol to three categories of people: customers under 18 years of age, drunks or customers acting in a disorderly fashion, and a police officer who is on duty.

The Licensing Act also requires the full holder of a justices' licence to display a notice stating the licensee's name and other details as required.

The Food Safety Act 1990

It is an offence to sell, or keep for eventual sale, food that:

– is unfit for human consumption or injurious to health; or
– is not of the nature, substance or quality demanded by the purchasers or falsely or misleadingly presented; or
– does not comply with food safety requirements.

The local authority officers have the power to enter the premises to investigate and inspect food as well as take samples for investigation. The Act also gives them power to make prohibition orders to enforce hygiene regulations and this can lead to premises being closed down, immediately if needed. Under the 1990 Act, the temperature for the storage of cooked foods was reduced to a maximum of 5°C for a number of categories of food including smoked or cured fish and meat, soft cheeses and cooked products containing meat, fish, and substances used as substitutes for meat, fish, eggs, cheeses or vegetables. Delivery vehicles will also have to deliver these foods with the 5°C requirement. The minimum temperature for hot food storage remains at 63°C.

The Food Premises (Registration) Regulations 1991 require all restaurants to register with their local district council. Registration is free and the local authority does not have the right to reject your application. Failure to register is a criminal offence which currently carries a maximum penalty of £400 on conviction. The giving of false information on a registration form currently carries a maximum fine of £2000.

The Act also lays down regulations requiring that kitchen staff receive practical hygiene training appropriate to their job. More details can be obtained from Food Sense, London SE99 7TT.

Consumer legislation

Turning away customers
Although the restaurateur has the right to turn away customers because of the dress code or the customers' behaviour, eg drunkenness, he or she has to be fully aware of the statutory restrictions imposed by the Sex Discrimination Act 1975 and the Race Relations Act 1976. It is unlawful discrimination to refuse service to a prospective customer on the grounds of either sex or race. It is strange to note, however, that a restaurateur may lawfully turn away a customer because of his political views, religion or homosexuality.

Theft Act 1978

Before the implementation of the Theft Act 1978, the law relating to customers walking out without paying was unclear. Section 3 of the Act states that it is an offence for a person to 'dishonestly make off without having paid as required or expected, and with intent to avoid payment of the amount due'. The Act also allows restaurants to arrest any customer suspected of committing the offence. However, if a customer is unable to pay because he hasn't got sufficient means to do so, but makes it clear that he intends to return to settle his bill, the restaurateur has no real power to arrest him.

Sale of Goods Act 1979

The food served has to correspond with the description; for instance, if you mention on your menu that there are shrimps in your seafood soup but you give king prawns instead, the customer is entitled to ask for his money back. The customer is not obliged to accept a replacement dish. The Act also requires food served to be of merchantable quality and fit for its purpose, ie fit for human consumption and of reasonable quality for the price paid.

Supply of Goods and Services Act 1982

The consumer is further protected by this Act if the food has not been served with 'reasonable care and skill', eg a perfectly edible T-bone steak which was overcooked or dropped on the floor by the waiter.

Trade Descriptions Act 1968

This Act covers dishonest description of food sold in terms of quality, method of preparation (eg 'home-made'), composition (eg '100 per cent vegetarian'), place and date of wine sold, advertisement and also description by the waiter when the order was taken.

Consumer Protection Act 1987

It is an offence to mislead consumers on prices. For example, if it is stated on the menu that prices are inclusive of VAT and service charge, it is an offence to add a further service charge to the bill.

The menu

What happens if the item selected from the menu is unavailable? Legally, a customer cannot demand that particular item as long as the waiter makes it clear, when the order is taken, that such an item is unavailable. In practice, most customers are happy to accept lack of availability as inevitable in a busy restaurant.

Safety and working conditions

General duty

The restaurateur is generally liable for injuries to his staff incurred during work. As an employer you have a general duty to ensure that all your employees are safe at work, especially those working in the kitchen. The general duty includes providing safe plant and equipment, a safe place of work, competent fellow employees and a safe system of work. The employer is also legally responsible for any injury caused by defective equipment, even though the defect is the fault of the manufacturer, but the employer could take action against the manufacturer. The kitchen staff have to be provided with protective clothing and must be properly trained and supervised.

Duties imposed by statute

Premises must be registered under the Offices, Shops and Railway Premises Act 1963 if there are any employees not in the owner's immediate family.

Health and Safety at Work Act 1974

There are two types of duty imposed by the Act, namely general duties and specific duties. The general duties basically state that: 'It shall be the duty of every employer to ensure, so far as is reasonably practicable, the health, safety and welfare at work of all his employees.' The specific duties require proper and adequate instructions to be given to the staff on exactly what procedures are to be followed to ensure safety at work.

Safety policy

There is a requirement for a written safety policy to be prepared where the restaurant has five or more staff. The policies should include:

- a general statement of the employer's commitment to ensure health and safety;
- the arrangements to ensure compliance with the required standards of health and safety at work;
- detailed reference to specific danger areas as well as first aid instructions. The Health and Safety Information for Employees Regulations 1989 require information relating to health and safety and welfare to be furnished to employees by means of an approved poster or leaflets which may be obtained from Her Majesty's Stationery Office.

It is an offence to mistreat the equipment provided to ensure health and safety, eg removing and misusing a fire extinguisher.

Where there are a number of staff whose command and understanding of English is poor, special measures have to be taken to explain the safety policy statement. Many restaurants which employ immigrant workers now have the safety policy written out in different languages.

Insurance against injuries

The Employers' Liability (Compulsory Insurance) Act 1969 requires restaurants to have valid and adequate cover for injury claims by employees. The insurance policy must cover bodily injury and disease resulting from working, and the cover must be at least £2 million. Any employer not insured in accordance with the Act is liable to heavy fines. A certificate of the insurance cover must be prominently displayed on the premises.

Fire safety

The Fire Precautions Act 1971 requires each restaurant to obtain a fire certificate, FP1. An application for the certificate has to be made to the local fire authority. To meet the requirements, the premises must:

- have adequate means of escape;
- be equipped with means of fire fighting;
- provide fire alarms and emergency lighting.

Staff must be drilled in the event of a fire and everyone in the kitchen must be instructed on the use of the different types of fire-fighting equipment; where kitchens employ staff for whom English is not the mother tongue, fire procedure and extinguisher operating instructions should be given in the appropriate languages.

Employment of children

There are strict rules when it comes to employing children. A child is defined by employment law as someone under the minimum school leaving age; in other words, under 16. You cannot employ anyone at all under the age of 13. Children over 13 can work part time, but are not allowed to work at the following times:

- Before 7am, and after 7pm
- During school hours when they are required to attend school
- For more than two hours on the days they are required to attend school
- For more than two hours on Sunday.

If you should decide to employ children, you will need to obtain a permit from the local education authority.

In the restaurant business, there are restrictions on employing people who are over 16 but under 18. It is illegal to employ a person under the age of 18 behind the bar. In the case of most restaurants, intoxicating liquor is ancillary to the meal. It is therefore permissible to employ such a person to serve intoxicating liquor with the meals provided the alcohol is obtained from a bar.

Music and the law

There are two licences which you have to apply for if you intend to have background music in your restaurant.

The Performing Right Society (PRS)

If copyright music is to be played in your restaurant (eg from tape or CD) you will need a PRS licence. The cost of a PRS licence depends on the type of premises being licensed, as the PRS has negotiated a variety of tariffs for all types of premises. You must get a PRS licence before music can be played and if you contact the Society for a licence before they contact you, you will receive a discount on your first year royalty. The address is:

The Performing Right Society Ltd
Copyright House
29–30 Berners Street
London W1P 4AA
Tel: 071-580 5544

Phonographic Performance Ltd

There are copyrights in recording and films which are separate from the copyright in the music itself; therefore, you will also need a licence from Phonographic Performance Ltd (PPL), which looks after the public performance of sound recording. Should you play video recordings, a licence is also required from Video Performance Ltd (VPL).

The address of PPL and VPL is:

Ganton House
14–22 Ganton Street
London W1V 1LB
Tel: 071-437 0311

Chapter 10

Food and Drinks Management

The purchase of food and drink is one of the most important aspects of managing a restaurant. A well-organised buyer can help a restaurant to save money. A good buyer must know all the ingredients used in the menu as well as be able to shop around and bargain for the best prices.

Control over food and beverage will depend on the size of the restaurant. For an owner-operated restaurant, there is usually no need to have sophisticated management controls as the owner himself will be involved in the purchasing. However, for larger ventures the objective of having good food and beverage management controls is to enable proper analysis of income and expenditure as well as to help in the pricing of the menu. Good controls can also ensure quality control over the purchase as well as prevent wastage and even fraud by the staff.

Purchasing system

The implementation of a good purchasing system is important. To develop a good system, the buyer must have knowledge of purchases required. One method is to prepare a checklist of all the raw materials, and for the chef to make periodical stock checks to see what purchases are necessary. The buyer must also know the current prices as well as the main sources for all the items.

Always ensure that deliveries are not made to the restaurant during the busy periods, and ideally only when the restaurant is not yet open for business. This will avoid having any of your staff awaiting deliveries and checking invoices instead of giving their full attention to the customers. Deliveries also tend to make a lot of noise unacceptable to the dining area.

When deliveries arrive, they must be checked thoroughly to ensure that everything that has been ordered is there and, more importantly, that it is of the required quality and quantity. Always check the sell-by date for cans and beers as it is not uncommon for suppliers to include some old stock. Make it a policy to check all the items delivered and tick off each one. This will ensure that all goods ordered have been delivered. The person responsible for checking these items must ensure that the goods are free from contamination and that canned goods are not damaged or rusty. Goods rejected must be clearly identified and set aside for return. To complete the control, the staff who did the checking will have to initial the delivery note. The delivery note should then be filed immediately, so that further matching can be done to the purchase invoice which usually arrives days, if not weeks, later. This will ensure that payment is only made for goods delivered.

Other points to consider when purchasing

1. Maintain good relations with trade representatives because they can supply useful, up-to-date information.
2. Keep a small number of suppliers to ease administration and control. However, always have two available suppliers for each product because competition among the suppliers will ensure quality goods at low prices.
3. Compare purchasing by retail and wholesale, and explore all possible suppliers; eg local markets, butchers. Though a cash and carry sells its products at considerably lower prices owing to bulk buying, there are usually many items which you can buy even cheaper from the supermarkets.
4. Consider using a computer system to help stock control (see Chapter 13).

Stock maintenance

An effective stock system must be implemented for the following reasons:

1. Maintenance of perishable products such as vegetables.

2. Control over the cost of food and beverage as well as loss because of pilferage and wastage.
3. As part of an effective purchasing system.
4. For insurance reasons in the event of a claim.

Stock maintenance techniques

Location. It is imperative that stock is well organised in the storage areas. Cans should be neatly stacked, and there must be room for perishables, eg vegetables, as well as neat non-food storage areas for napkins, glassware, aprons, invoices, order pads, candles etc. Small signs identifying each storage area will help to manage stocktaking more efficiently as well as help the staff to pinpoint the location of each product, especially when deliveries arrive. An ideal layout format is to have items used daily stored in an easily accessible location and the stocktaking list should be in the same order as the layout of the items stored.

Stocktaking. This has to be done periodically and as often as possible. Though stocktaking can be laborious and time-consuming, it is good practice to do it formally for a number of reasons:

1. To determine the amount and value of items at one particular point.
2. To compare with the book value to have control over pilferage and wastage.
3. To identify slow-moving stock so that special sales promotions can be made to sell these items before they perish.

Storage of food

It is essential that all food is stored in a cool and clean area, and it must be covered. For hygienic reasons, store all goods off the ground on racks or shelving of an impervious material. It is important that all the outer packings of goods are removed immediately from the food preparation area to avoid the risk of contamination. Raw food (eg meat and fish) has to be kept separate from cooked foods at all times. It is recommended that raw food is stored in a separate refrigerator. However, where there is limited storage space use the lowest shelves of a refrigerator for raw meats, but always remember to put the meat on a tray so as to prevent blood contaminating the refrigerator.

Where food is to be stored in a deep freezer, there are a number of rules to follow. Frozen food deliveries have to be transferred immediately to the freezer and not allowed to defrost. The freezer has to be maintained at $-22°C$. A freezer is intended for the storage of frozen foods, and if fresh food is to be frozen, it must be done properly in accordance with the manufacturer's instructions. Defrost and clean the freezer regularly.

How much stock of each item to keep will depend on an estimate of sales and volume in the coming period. Overstocking must be avoided because it ties up working capital and uses up space. With overstocking there is also a likelihood of greater wastage from deterioration as well as pilferage by staff. On the other hand, if stock levels are kept to a minimum, recording costs, eg delivery charges, will be incurred. There will also be unwanted extra administration and management time involved.

Minimum ordering quantities will result in lower trade discounts. Stock should always be kept on a first-in, first-out system (FIFO). This can only be properly maintained if the storage space is kept tidy and neat. In order to establish the optimum stock level, you need to be able to predict the volume of sales for a period. To do so you must be able to forecast the total number of customers and the choice of menu items.

Sales and volume forecasting is not as difficult or scientific as it sounds because forecasting can be based on past experience. Therefore, it is important to keep good records of the numbers of each dish sold.

Production control

Production control is required to ensure that the cost and amount of items used from stock is consistent with the total number of meals sold. The cost of this food consumed will depend on the number of each menu item produced and the cost per menu item. One method of control is to cross-reference the items on the waiters' and waitresses' ordering pads to the kitchen production records. This will prevent the staff keeping the cash sales and destroying the order pad as the kitchen production records have to tally exactly with the orders taken. The kitchen production records are then checked with the goods issued from stock. The cost of the goods issued from stock should approximate to the food production costs, the latter being calculated from the number of menu items and estimated cost per item. If each element of the system tallies with the others, management can be confident that all food usage and costs are being properly recorded.

Chapter 11
Fitting Out the Restaurant

Design and layout of the kitchen

There must be adequate space in the kitchen for the staff to work safely and efficiently. The ideal kitchen should enable food to be prepared and served as efficiently as possible as well as ensuring kitchen hygiene. The kitchen has to be large enough to allow the following activities:

- Preparation and cooking of food
- Washing up
- Storage of food and equipment
- Refuse and sanitary storage
- Ease of supervision.

The premises have to be arranged so that dirty and clean operations are separated. It is also important that cooked food is kept separate from raw food.

The kitchen environment
The Offices, Shops and Railway Premises Act 1963 requires 400 cubic feet per person. Provision for the replacement of extracted air with fresh air is important as a humid atmosphere is ideal for bacteria to breed and unpleasant to work in. The temperature should not be higher than 25°C for the comfort of staff, otherwise work will be impaired.

Floors, walls and ceilings
The best floor surface is non-slip ceramic tiling as this provides a smooth, non-absorbent, hard-wearing surface which is easy to clean. Health and safety legislation requires that such a surface be provided in all areas where food is prepared. PVC tiles are commonly used but, if they are not

laid properly, dirt will accumulate between the joints and under ill-fitting tiles.

For the walls, smooth, impervious and easy-to-clean surfaces are best. Any structural dampness must be eliminated and all walls adjacent to food preparation surfaces and sinks must be able to withstand heat, moisture and impact. It is important that joints and edges are sealed to prevent dirt accumulating. Kitchen ceilings must also be fireproof.

Washing facilities and water supplies

A stainless steel, double-bowl sink is important for effective washing up by hand. A separate sink is also required for preparing food. The kitchen must have a hand-wash basin which is easily accessible. Every basin should have hot and cold water, a nail brush, soap, and towels or dryer. The cold water supply must be from the mains. Water storage tanks should be accessible and always kept clean to prevent contamination. There should be an instant supply of hot water.

Lighting and ventilation

Adequate lighting is necessary for safe working conditions. Proper lighting is also required by the Health and Safety Act to detect dust. A rough guideline is as follows:

	Fluorescent	Tungsten
Food preparation areas	30 watts/square metre	150 watts/square metre
Storage areas	6 watts/square metre	30 watts/square metre

Adequate ventilation is essential to prevent heat, steam and grease condensing on the walls and ceilings as well as to remove smells. The ventilation system should be able to replace extracted air with fresh air. If the restaurant is in a residential area or operates outside normal working hours, there are additional requirements to avoid causing noise and smells. Noise hoods and fans must be kept clean; grease and dust are drawn up by the fan and if they accumulate, can be a fire hazard.

Refuse

A refuse storage area should be provided separate from the storage and handling rooms. The area must have adequate drainage and should have a hard, non-absorbent surface. A close-fitting lid must also be used on each refuse container. It is recommended that a waste disposal unit is installed under a sink as it is convenient, clean and tidy. It is against the law to burn any waste on the premises. All restaurants must have an agreement with the local council or, more likely, a private contractor with regard to refuse collection.

Personal hygiene

The chefs and all the kitchen staff must be constantly reminded of the measures to promote personal hygiene. Personal hygiene can prevent contamination. You are responsible for providing changing and sanitary facilities as well as written notices instructing the staff to wash their hands after using the toilet. The kitchen staff must be told to bandage cuts and sores with waterproof dressings and also to wear clean clothing. Smoking should be banned in any room where food is being prepared. It is also important to show kitchen staff the correct and hygienic way to taste food.

Kitchen clothing

Kitchen staff must wear suitable clothing and footwear. Suitable clothing must protect the legs from being scalded or burnt. A chef's hat has to be worn to prevent loose hairs from dropping into food and to absorb sweat. Lightweight disposable hats are now commonly used. Modern industrial safety shoes should be worn. Kitchen clothing should also be light and comfortable as well as washable and absorbent.

First aid

A proper first aid kit must be provided. The Health and Safety (First Aid) Regulations 1981 list a summary of requirements for restaurants with up to 50 employees.

No of items	No of employees		
	1–5	6–10	11–50
Guidance card	1	1	1
Sterile eye pad	1	2	4
Triangular bandages	1	2	4
Sterile coverings for serious wounds	1	2	4
Safety pins	6	6	12
Medium-sized sterile unmedicated dressings	3	6	8
Large sterile unmedicated dressings	1	2	4
Extra large sterile unmedicated dressings	1	2	4
Individually wrapped sterile adhesive dressings	10	20	40

Kitchen equipment

The type and range of kitchen equipment will depend on the type of cuisine being served. When you move into an already fitted restaurant, obviously you will find the basic kitchen equipment already installed, eg ovens, grills etc. But there are a number of points which you will need to consider carefully when choosing your own equipment. Commercial kitchen equipment is expensive, yet unreliable equipment can bring the kitchen to a standstill. You should note:

- Overall dimension in relation to available space and ergonomic design.
- Overall quality and whether the equipment falls within the gas or electricity board regulations.
- Fuel type and whether the existing supply is adequate.
- Capacity – can the equipment handle all the cooking? – and the convenience of handling.

- Compatibility with other equipment and whether the floor can support the weight.
- Maintenance and ease of handling and cleaning as well as mobility.
- Overall cost including the initial price, running costs, number of years before replacement and insurance costs.

Type of material

Stainless steel

This is the most common material because of its durability, strength and ease of cleaning. There are many different types of stainless steel and the best for food is known as 18:8, which represents an alloy of steel with chromium and nickel making up 18 and 8 per cent of its composition. The disadvantages of stainless steel are the noise generated when you work with it and its relatively poor thermal conductivity.

Copper

Copper has a high thermal conductivity which makes it suitable for cooking equipment. As copper can be dissolved by acidic food, catering equipment made from copper is usually lined with tin. However, do make sure that the lead content in the tinned copper cooking utensils is minimal, as recent research has showed that lead can be absorbed by foods which in the long term can be harmful to health. Putting a pan on a large flame without fat or liquid can damage the tin lining and retinning is expensive.

Aluminium

Equipment made from aluminium is suitable for many cooking processes because it is strong, of heavy construction and does not tarnish. However, aluminium can be expensive. Another disadvantage is that other metals have to be added to it to make the equipment stronger as aluminium is a soft metal. This can result in certain foods becoming discoloured. Wooden rather than metal utensils should be used with aluminium pans, otherwise aluminium will be present in the food. Research suggests that this is harmful to health.

Non-stick metal
Many kitchen utensils are now made of non-stick metal. However, non-stick metal utensils cannot withstand excessive heat and scratch easily, thus losing their non-stick properties.

Main items

Ovens
Convection ovens. A motorised fan forces hot air around a convection oven, thus ensuring a constant temperature. Heat is used efficiently, so a shorter time is required for cooking. However, one disadvantage of forced convection ovens is that food quickly becomes dry.

Microwave ovens. These are becoming more popular. Microwave ovens use a high frequency of power. Most have turntables which ensure that the food is consistently exposed to the microwaves. They are especially useful in preheating just before serving. Microwave ovens have to be cleaned thoroughly all the time because spilled food can reduce efficiency. They are also useful for cooking vegetables and defrosting. One disadvantage is that they do not brown the food.

Combined microwave and convection ovens. The combined properties of forced convection and microwaves are very effective; microwaves heat the food from inside while forced convection browns the outside.

Steamers. There are two types of steaming oven: atmospheric and pressure. The atmospheric steamer uses natural convection steam at 100 per cent. This produces high quality steamed food but one disadvantage is the length of time needed. Pressure steamers take less time and are more efficient.

Deep fat fryers
These can be found in most, if not all, restaurant kitchens. Deep fat fryers should have a thermostat to control the

temperature. Most fryers are internally heated with electric immersion elements. There is a cool zone where the oil is cooler and where food particles can sink without burning. This will prevent food being spoiled as well as prolonging the useful life of the oil. Pressurised fryers use an air-tight frying vat which enables food to be cooked faster as well as saving fuel cost.

Hot cupboards

Hot cupboards are used to store cooked food as well as to heat serving dishes and plates. You have to ensure that the heat of the hot cupboard is controlled at a reasonable temperature (65–85°C). Though a hot cupboard is useful for keeping food warm, be aware that food loses its flavour and texture if stored for too long there.

Bains maries are holding units for foods in open wells of water used for keeping food hot. You have to ensure that the *bain marie* is never allowed to burn dry.

Cold storage

The amount of cold storage required will depend on the size of the restaurant and menu. Although most restaurants can manage with several refrigerators, deep freeze cabinets and thermostatically controlled cabinets, larger restaurants may need to have cold rooms. This type of walk-in fridge is designed so that it is divided into separate compartments, where meat is kept separate from deep frozen foods.

Mechanical equipment

Food mixers

These are labour-saving, electrically operated machines used for a wide variety of purposes including mixing pastry, beating egg whites, mincing, slicing or chopping vegetables and meat. It is best to buy an all-purpose mixer with a full selection of attachments. It is important that all the components are washed and dried after use, and that there is no rust. The mixers must also be lubricated frequently.

Food slicers

Food slicers come with variable speeds to allow for different requirements. They can be dangerous if not operated properly, so it is important that kitchen staff know how to use them. Working instructions should be placed in a prominent position so that all users can read them. The blades must be sharpened regularly and the mixers lubricated frequently.

Liquidisers

These are especially useful for mixing fresh spices and blending foods. Liquidisers must be cleaned properly after each use. Though a domestic liquidiser may be adequate, it is recommended that a commercial liquidiser is used.

Peelers

Peelers are used to peel root vegetables, especially potatoes. Although ready-peeled vegetables are now available, the demand for freshly prepared vegetables is a prerequisite for a quality restaurant. Whether the peelers are bench or floor mounted, it is important that the waste discharge is received at the proper place. Either the sink into which the waste is discharged should be fitted with a strainer or the waste should be discharged straight into the automatic waste disposal unit.

Checklist of small utensils

Basic cutting utensils

- Knives for trimming, slicing and chopping
- Filleting and boning knives
- Peeler
- Choppers and cleavers
- Cutting boards
- Meat saw

Cooking utensils

- Frying pan
- Sauté pan
- Stewing pan

- Large pots
- Roasting trays
- Grilling trays
- Colander
- Vegetable drainer
- Frying basket
- Kettle

Other small utensils

- Whisks
- Wooden/plastic spoons
- Serving spoons
- Grilling tongs
- Skimmer
- Can openers
- Bottle openers
- Cutlery containers
- Rolling pins
- Scales
- Thermometers
- Kitchen scissors
- Sieves
- Spatulas
- Timers.

Restaurant furniture

The fixtures and fittings of the restaurant will largely depend on the type of cuisine as well as on how much you plan to spend. Although it is not advisable to over-spend on furniture, customers will be more attracted to a well-decorated restaurant than one which is badly furnished.

Tables and chairs

The tables and chairs have to be compatible, both in style and dimension. There should be a range of tables from two to six covers to allow the most efficient use of available seating. Round tables are advantageous as they can seat more people, but remember that round tables cannot be linked with other tables should large groups of customers turn up. Chairs have to be comfortable and durable. The width must allow the chairs to be pushed under the table without getting in the way of the table legs.

Toilets

The Environmental Health Department has laid down minimum requirements with respect to sanitary accommodation. For instance, you will need one urinal and one washbasin per 50 customers. There must also be a ventilated lobby between the toilet and any area where there is food. The doors to the lavatories must shut by themselves and extractor fans are recommended. A 'Wash Your Hands' notice must be displayed prominently in every toilet used by the staff.

Chapter 12

Day-to-day Running of the Restaurant

Good planning and organisation are essential if the restaurant is to run smoothly and successfully. Lack of order and routine will have a detrimental effect on the food and service. The wrong ingredients might be ordered, and meals might be served late or lukewarm by a poorly trained waitress. The customer will not have an enjoyable time and will not return.

When you begin the daily preparation of the restaurant will depend on the opening time. A restaurant that opens for lunch or all day will need to start early in the morning. The type of food served will obviously affect how much food preparation is necessary; a fast food restaurant serving convenience food will have less to prepare in advance than a restaurant serving freshly cooked and inventive meals. Most restaurants start work at least two hours before opening to enable the kitchen staff to prepare the food and be ready for the first orders.

Good planning and preparation have their rewards. It is satisfying to devise and plan the menu and service, and see it all successfully materialise. And, of course, the customers will be satisfied too.

The kitchen

Most rules for the kitchen are common sense. They ensure that food quality is of a good standard, and that the kitchen staff work in a safe and orderly environment. The kitchen must be neat and organised with the equipment and raw material in the right places.

Food preparation

The most commonly used method is the *partie system*, where the kitchen is subdivided into separate areas depending on the type of food being cooked. The head chef should have overall control of the kitchen with assistant chefs (sous chefs) under him.

Preparation of food has to be carefully planned and staff well trained. Inefficient preparation of raw materials and too much wastage will affect the restaurant's profitability.

Raw food must be kept separate from cooked food or food that does not need cooking. This is to prevent bacteria from the raw food contaminating other food. Separate work surfaces, equipment and utensils should be used for raw food. If the same work surface has to be used owing to shortage of space, use separate chopping boards. Food should be kept covered until ready to serve or be collected.

Thawing frozen food

Meat and some other foods must be thoroughly thawed before it is cooked otherwise the food will not be cooked completely through, and bacteria may not be killed. Food poisoning bacteria begin to multiply once the thawed food reaches 4°C, so do not hold food above this temperature before it is cooked. Thawed liquid from the food must be disposed of and not allowed to contaminate other food.

Safe cooking

To ensure adequate cooking, all food must be heated until its centre reaches above 70°C. A probe thermometer should be inserted into the food/oven to see if the food has reached the right temperature.

Food must be cooked for the correct amount of time according to its type and the quantity being cooked. Slight variations may be allowed to cater for customers who request that their meat is slightly rare or well done. Special care must be taken when using a microwave – the manufacturer's instructions should be followed exactly.

Storage and reheating of cooked food

Cooked food should be stored below 4°C or above 70°C to prevent bacterial growth. If a large pot of stock is required, keep it simmering until it is needed. If the quantity of stock is large, there is a danger that it may not completely heat through. Bacteria multiply in the cooler areas, so always cook the stock long enough and stir frequently.

If the food is to be refrigerated after cooking, cool the food as quickly as possible before placing it in the refrigerator to prevent bacterial growth. The food should be kept below 4°C at all times.

When cooked chilled food is re-heated, the centre must reach 70°C to destroy all bacteria. Leftovers must be disposed of completely and on no account should the food be re-heated and used again.

The dining area

Efficiency, advance preparation, hygiene and comfort are the watchwords for the dining area. Much activity goes on here, but good rules will create a relaxed atmosphere.

Daily duties

Draw up a list of duties which the waiters and waitresses are expected to perform before opening times. The following duties are recommended.

- Ensure that all the tables are laid out, and new candles in place
- Sweep and tidy the dining area
- Ensure that the bar area is clean and tidy
- Warm up the dining area in cold weather
- Ensure that the bar is adequately stocked
- Fill up the ice buckets and cut up lemon slices
- Polish the mirrors and other shiny surfaces
- Update the menu for the day (if applicable)
- Stock sideboards with spare cutlery
- If advance bookings have been made, allocate and reserve tables accordingly
- Clean ashtrays should be available

- Clean the customers' toilets and provide sufficient soap, paper and towels
- Check periodically that the toilets are clean during opening hours as many customers judge a restaurant's hygiene by the state of the conveniences.

Ventilation

Good ventilation is necessary for several reasons:

- to prevent a humid atmosphere caused by cooking and body heat
- to disperse food smells
- to maintain fresh air for the comfort of the diners.

Air conditioning is ideal as it can be used to heat or cool the room. If air conditioning is not possible, ventilate the area by opening the windows or ventilation grilles or doors or using extractor fans. Do, however, make sure that there is no draught near the diners. Note that 1000 cubic feet of air per person per hour are required.

Smoking

Many customers who do not smoke object to dining near smokers, especially since the dangers of passive smoking have become more apparent. You should seriously consider providing separate smoking and non-smoking areas. When designing or refurbishing the dining area, stronger ventilation should be provided for smoking areas.

Serving the customers

Good service means setting the customer at ease and meeting all his or her needs. Good service enhances the customer's meal experience (see Chapter 6). The waiters and waitresses should be carefully selected (see Chapter 8) and should be polite, personable and quick.

When the customer enters there should be a waiter or waitress ready to welcome him (or her) and show him to a suitable table. If there is no table available, seat the customer, estimate the waiting time, and offer a drink or nibbles. The waiter should offer to take the customer's coat and accessories if storage space is available. (A notice disclaiming responsibility for damage or loss to the belongings should be displayed.)

Once the customer is seated, present him with the menu and inform him about any special offers or the soup of the day. Ask whether a drink is required, and allow him some time to read the menu on his own. When you return to take the order, always be ready and willing to recommend dishes or explain what is in them. Read out the order to check that it is correct.

The dish should be served as soon as possible and the diner should be allowed to taste the wine before a full glass is poured. At some point the waiter should return to check that everything is agreeable and to refill the wine glass.

The customer should have a 'breathing space' between courses to allow food to settle, but he should not be left to wait too long. Much can be learnt from the customer's body language as to whether he is impatient or not in a hurry.

Plates should be collected a short while after the last diner at a table has finished. If necessary, brush crumbs off the table quickly but unobtrusively. Ask whether the customer would like a dessert or a coffee or liqueur. A complimentary mint or chocolate with the coffee creates a good impression.

The customer should never be made to feel rushed, even if it is nearing or past closing time. If the customer stays ludicrously beyond closing time or his last order, the bill may be discreetly presented, but at all other times the bill should only be given when requested. Place it face down, preferably on a special plate, and next to the customer who is entertaining the other diner or diners. If it is not apparent who is the entertainer, place the bill between the diners.

Controlling the day's takings

For the restaurant to survive, you must make a profit. Turnover needs to be high, and stealing by staff eliminated. The daily takings are a measure of how well you are meeting the customers' needs. The takings will vary according to the day of the week. If you notice that the takings are particularly down on one day of the week on a regular basis, this may be the day to make special offers.

Profit can be lost by staff stealing the takings. The best method of prevention is the physical presence of the restaurateur and his close involvement in the running of the restaurant. Staff should be made aware that theft is a criminal offence and offenders will be dealt with severely. Various controls to reduce theft may be used:

1. Use pre-numbered duplicated order pads; each waiter has his own pad.
2. Use pre-numbered sales invoices, and make a note of the type of payment (credit card, cash or cheque) received on the invoice.
3. Use a separate order pad for drinks orders.
4. Reconcile the total orders against the number of dishes cooked.
5. Reconcile the daily takings with till rolls or invoices.
6. Record the daily takings promptly (see Chapter 5).

Sufficient denominations of coins and notes must be available so that change can be given. You will probably need to visit your bank or post office frequently.

Closing up

Meals have been eaten, drinks drunk, and the customers have left, contented after an enjoyable experience and inclined to return. This is a satisfying time of day, but the place is in a mess and much needs to be done to get the show on the road again for the evening opening hours or the following day. Chores will include:

● Cleaning, setting and laying tables
● Restocking sideboards
● Reconciliation of cash with the till rolls
● Attending to the cash float
● Cleaning.

It is important to sort out the cash reconciliation at the end of any one shift, especially if there is a changeover of staff. If errors are spotted promptly, the relevant staff can be easily identified for questioning.

Cleaning is also important but routine. Draw up a list of cleaning duties so that individual staff are sure of their responsibilities and can get started on them as soon as the restaurant closes. If special cleaning staff are used, they should be told what needs to be done. For hygiene and safety, the correct detergents at the correct concentration should be used for the appropriate surfaces. Staff should be familiar with the correct procedure.

The day-to-day running of a restaurant may seem exhausting, and it is certainly hard work, but a good routine will help to ensure that everything which needs to be done is done in the minimum time. Attention to the detail of the daily routine is what distinguishes a professional from an amateur.

Chapter 13
Other Matters

Computers

Computers are becoming more and more popular in the restaurant business. This is largely because of the technological advances over the last few years, which have brought the prices of powerful microcomputers down to affordable levels. But many restaurateurs are put off computers by the technical jargon.

A computer can be regarded as being made up of three parts: the hardware (the computer itself), the software (programs to run the computer) and the final products (eg printed invoices, stock ledgers). The use of a computer can provide better management controls for the running of the restaurant, and can help to produce timely management accounts, up-to-date stock records, impressive word processing etc. Nevertheless, one has to be careful when implementing a new computer system because the staff operating the system must be properly trained.

It is all too common for the proprietor of a business to assume that the computer will solve every problem when in fact, if the computer has been used incorrectly, important information can be lost and time and money wasted trying to put things right. Moreover, it is sometimes unwise to input every scrap of information regarding the restaurant because the last thing you want is that confidential information should be accessible by staff.

Uses of the computer
One of the most common uses is to computerise the accounting system. There are programs for payroll records, purchase ledgers, nominal ledgers (recording all your income and expenditure) and also stock control. Many

restaurants now use computerised electronic cash registers which produce invoices listing all the items. The use of the computerised cash register will enable analysis of sales into subsections, eg starters, main courses, desserts and drinks.

Computers can also help in planning because there are programs which will not only record which dish was sold, but also the number of times it was sold, as well as the time of day when it was sold.

A computer can be used in the design and production of the menu. There are many user-friendly desktop publishing programs to update and produce your menus, allowing you to introduce new dishes and change menus easily. The desktop publishing programs available are advanced enough to enable you to do your own graphics and artwork, which is much cheaper than paying for professional printing.

Expansion

When the restaurant has become established and business is thriving, you may feel that it is time to expand, move into a larger restaurant or even open a second. Experience in the booming 1980s saw many successful restaurants acquiring new premises and opening new restaurants. However, many of these restaurants have reconsolidated their position and shut most, if not all, of their off-shoot restaurants, retaining only the original one. One of the main reasons is, of course, the recession which hit in the 1990s.

One problem with expansion is that you cannot be as closely involved as you can with just one restaurant. As the appeal of most owner-run restaurants depends on the presence and personality of the owner, running more than one restaurant can have detrimental effects. Also, you will not have the same tight management controls over the running of your restaurant because you will need to delegate much of the work to your managers or partners. Often with the opening of new branches, new partners have to be brought in. This, naturally, has disadvantages, as you will have to consult with someone else on the running of the restaurant. If, however, you can resolve these problems, expansion into larger premises or more restaurants will certainly bring you more wealth.

Other ways of expanding the business

Take-away

This is a sensible spin-off from your restaurant, as take-aways can function with existing equipment and staff. Do not underestimate trade from take-away business as there is less need to worry about service and the 'meal experience' of the take-away customers. In other words, the same money can be earned with less expense and effort.

Having a take-away service will help to reach a larger proportion of the public as many people like to eat their food in the comfort of their own homes, in front of the television. When the take-away customers are happy with the food, it is likely that they will return as sit-in customers. Many restaurants now offer a free take-away delivery service. There is no doubt that this appeals to a large section of the population, as delivery service has now become standard, though at present it is more applicable to pizzas, Indian and Chinese food.

Take-away business can also be used as a marketing technique by using attractive and eye-catching packaging. It is a good idea to have your restaurant's logo and telephone number on the take-away boxes.

Another point to consider is the pricing of the take-away menu. Many restaurants have discounts on take-aways. Some have special take-away menus which only offer dishes which do not require a lot of preparation. This is a good idea because, no matter how lucrative the take-away business may be, you must never let the service and quality of food served to your sit-in customers be affected by the take-away trade. If the restaurant is packed and the kitchen staff are under pressure, the only sensible thing to do is to turn away the take-away customers or tell them that their order will take much longer because of your busy period. As many take-away orders are taken over the telephone, many restaurants leave the telephone off the hook at busy times.

Private catering

Private catering is another way of expanding without having to buy new equipment. This is a lucrative business, as you can work out the profitability of each event before agreeing to it. The food can also be prepared in the kitchen when it is not being used for daily food preparation.

You will find that, as the restaurant becomes better known and acquires a good reputation for its food, more people will ask the restaurant to cater for special events. These will range from simply preparing a number of dishes to feeding hundreds of people in exhibition halls. When the latter occurs, you will need to employ more staff just for the event. With each successful venture, the reputation of the restaurant will grow and this can only help the business in the long run.

Pest control

All restaurants should have a properly drawn up contract with a pest contractor, who is both reliable and reputable. It is imperative that the design and construction of the restaurant premises should enable the elimination of vermin.

To prevent problems with vermin, the following is recommended:

● Provide close-fitting vermin-proof doors and windows
● Ensure that containers for the storage of food have tight-fitting lids
● In the planning of bars, shelves and other storage rooms, make sure that there are no inaccessible areas or spaces
● Removable furniture is preferable to fixed bench seating
● Ensure that there is adequate stock control, eg stock rotation and disposal of rotten food.

Noise control

This is especially relevant if the restaurant is in a residential area. Noise pollution is caused by noise from ventilation, music, live entertainment and commotion from customers leaving the premises. Different councils have different guidelines but in general the following requirements should be noted:

- Noise from any equipment and plant used in the restaurant should not increase the ambient noise level, measured outside the windows of any adjacent premises by more than two decibels.
- When the premises are being refurbished, adequate plans and proposals should be incorporated to ensure that effective noise and vibration control measures are employed.

Cutting energy costs

One of the largest elements of the running costs of a restaurant is the electricity and gas expenses. It is therefore important to lay down some rules on how to reduce energy consumption, especially in the kitchen. Make a practice of switching equipment, heat and lights off when not in use. In the kitchen, instruct the staff to switch off kitchen appliances when they are finished with them. Ventilators should only be run at the maximum level if essential. Doors of ovens and refrigerators should be open for as short a time as possible. Refrigerators should be properly defrosted. All equipment should be checked and maintained frequently, eg insulation of boilers, repairs to leaking taps and frequent cleaning of ventilator filters.

Chapter 14

A Case Study

This chapter was written by the author's brother, Dennis Sim, who runs a restaurant in west London.

Conception

The decision to start a restaurant began with a longing to escape the drudgery of air-conditioned offices and try something more exciting and rewarding. Capital and experience were lacking but enthusiasm was plentiful.

Every weekend a group of friends and I discussed the possibilities of making an enormous amount of money. This was usually done over a sumptuous meal. Everyone offered a quick verbal curriculum vitae – and it was discovered that more than half knew how to cook. As the others were self-confessed gastronomes it was decided that the catering business should be the 'sideline'! Little did we know that it would soon absorb our every moment!

Gestation period

Full of enthusiasm, we started looking for a restaurant. Many properties were found, as England was in the depths of recession. Existing restaurants with declining sales were going cheap, but an unwelcome premium on the business was always a deterrent to a virtually non-existent capital base. A modest sum of money was available from friends and family but was not enough to start up a property in a 'shell' condition – a place which needs total refurbishment.

After going through newspapers, estate agent mail-outs and contact with business transfer agencies – not to mention clocking up mileage in and around London – we finally came up with the 'ideal' situation. What was needed was an existing restaurant, with all the equipment and fittings, which we could rent. 'Ah! A management buy-out!', exclaimed one of the accountants in the gang.

A restaurant with 750 square feet and 32 covers was found in west London. The owners were approached and the terms negotiated. Lawyers were called in. We were in business.

Ante-natal exercises

So much to prepare, and so little time to do it in: construction of the menu, printing of the menu, invoices, printing advertising 'flyers', acquiring the equipment and perishables needed.

As we had a shoe-string budget, we looked for second-hand items, but added an individual touch with decorations. Our restaurant is mostly Malaysian, so we looked for decorations with a Far Eastern influence.

There was a mood of great expectancy when we moved into the restaurant – everyone helped to do up the restaurant and the recipes for the dishes were fine-tuned. All possible preparations were made in the kitchen in anticipation of the grand opening night. An advertisement was placed in the local newspaper, offering a 10 per cent discount for a limited period. But would the customers come?

The birth

The restaurant opened at half past six in the evening. For two hours there was only one table of a couple, who enjoyed a carefully prepared meal. But by about 8 pm, the restaurant was full! The restaurant was moving at full steam. There were groups of various sizes to accommodate and needs of various kinds to meet. Mistakes were made and salutary lessons were quickly learnt. But the customers seemed to enjoy themselves. When the doors shut, we were both exhausted and exhilarated.

After the first night, we sat round a table and decided that many systems had to be improved. The restaurant is based on two floors with the ground floor as the serving area and the kitchen in the basement, so communication had to be improved. A dumb waiter or a lift for food was used to transport food. Sophisticated methods of passing messages were used, ie shouting via the dumb waiter! An electrical internal communication system was needed. Even more tired but still excited, we got ready for more business.

Growing up

As time passed, we slowly fine-tuned the system implemented and improved customer service. We learnt more about ourselves as each of us was pushed to the limits of physical and mental capacity. We employed extra staff to ease this as well as to increase sales levels. The menu was adjusted to suit the local palate, as some spicy food not only whets customers' appetite for more drinks, it changes their normally placid composure to one of euphoria. Another important consideration was the employment of staff. The interviewing process is crucial to the selection of appropriate personnel. Training and general consideration for staff welfare are equally important.

Adolescence

Busy periods were noted so that we were prepared for the sudden arrival of large numbers of customers. It always seemed that they made prior arrangements among themselves to dine at the same time without letting us know! Valentine's day, month ends and weekends were especially busy.

Adulthood

There were obvious lessons to be learnt, and we have all aged prematurely by about 20 years! We are considering expanding to bigger premises or even starting a chain of restaurants. A delivery service is in the planning process and gradual changes to the menu to accommodate changing customer tastes are being implemented.

Now that we have matured, we have our own 'secret recipes' and some dishes are so popular they have become a trademark. Authenticity and quality are our mottoes as well as, of course, the customer is always right. Fortunately, the customer seems always to come back, so we must be doing something right. I hope to see you there one day!

Further Reading from Kogan Page

The Business Plan Workbook, 2nd edition, Colin Barrow, Paul Barrow and Robert Brown, 1992

The Catering Management Handbook, Judy Ridgway and Brian Ridgway, 1994

Financial Management for the Small Business: The Daily Telegraph Guide, 2nd edition, 1988

Forming a Limited Company, 4th edition, Patricia Clayton, 1994

Running Your Own Catering Company, Judy Ridgway, 1992

Taking Up a Franchise, 10th edition, Colin Barrow and Godfrey Golzen, 1993 (annual)

Working for Yourself: The Daily Telegraph Guide to Self-Employment, 15th edition, Godfrey Golzen, 1994

Index

Solicitors 16, 62, 66, 75
Staff
  children 81
  clothing 40
  communication 73
  fire procedures 81
  first aid 90
  Health and Safety at Work
    Act *1974*, *1978* 69, 79, 89
  Health and Safety
    Information for Employers
    Regulations *1989* 80
  hygiene 90
  incentive schemes 74
  insurance 80
  motivation and morale 73
  Offices, Shops and Railway
    Premises Act *1963* 79
  pilfering by 87
  policies 74
  recruitment 72–3
  relations with owner 73
  safety 79, 80
  statutory rights 69–70
Stationery 24–5
Stock maintenance 84–5
Supply of Goods and Services
  Act *1982* 78
Surveyors 64

Take-aways 107
  alcohol 76
  VAT 40
Takings 102–4
Tax
  income tax 71, 72
  National Insurance 23, 48, 69, 72
  PAYE 23, 48, 69, 71
  payroll bureaux 48
  reducing tax 64
  New Employer's Starter Pack 48, 71
  VAT 23, 39–41, 78
Theft Act *1978* 78
Toilets 97
Trade credits 30
Trade Descriptions Act *1968* 78

Value added tax 39–41
Video Performance Ltd 82

Waiters
  appearance of 56, 101–2
  behaviour 56
  casual labour 69
  recruitment 73
  serving food 56, 101–2
  training 56, 101–2